MY TEACHER, MY FUTURE

Indiana's Best and Brightest Remember Their Favorite Teacher

Compiled by Robert J. Krajewski, Ed.D.

Edited by Susan Baker

My Teacher, My Future: Indiana's Best and Brightest Remember
Their Favorite Teacher
Copyright © 2010
Robert J. Krajewski, Ed.D.

Library of Congress Control Number: 2010920888
ISBN: 978-0-615-33992-4
First printing: February 2010 – 1000 copies

FOR INFORMATION CONTACT:
Dr. Robert J. Krajewski, Ed.D.
Educational Research Foundation of Indiana, Inc.
P.O. Box 3182
Munster, IN 46321 * pzz@gate.net

Printed in the United States by Morris Publishing®
3212 East Highway 30
Kearney, NE 68847
1-800-650-7888

ACKNOWLEDGEMENTS

Many thanks to Dr. Charles Costa and his staff at the Northern Indiana Education Service Center for assistance in gathering data for "My Teacher, My Future" and distributing it to school libraries.

To Jeff Hamilton for the book's layout and design.

To Philip Potempa, columnist for the Northwest Indiana Times, for his invaluable aid in establishing contacts.

To our contributors for submitting anecdotes sometimes humorous, sometimes heartwarming, but always entertaining.

To John P. Newton, now vice president of the Indiana State University Foundation and former executive director of the Indiana State University Alumni Association, for facilitating contacts with ISU alumni.

To my editor, the talented, experienced and aggressive Susan Baker. She continually encouraged, pushed and prodded me to do my part towards the book's completion. Heartfelt thanks, Susan!

Robert J. Krajewski, Ed.D.
Educational Research Foundation of Indiana, Inc.

INTRODUCTION

"My Teacher, My Future: Indiana's Best and Brightest Remember Their Favorite Teacher" is a tribute to the teachers of yesterday who have educated and guided the professionals of today. It's a collection of memories about favorite teachers from influential Hoosiers – people who are the best and brightest in the fields of science, sports, entertainment, education, medicine, government service, philanthropy and more.

The goal of "My Teacher, My Future" is to reach out to students who are undecided about their future and encourage them to consider education as a career choice. Research has shown that too few of our most talented youngsters choose education as a career path. Perhaps realizing the lasting impact one teacher can have will encourage more students to strongly consider majoring in the field of education.

The favorite teachers honored here labored in classrooms from kindergarten through graduate school and include athletic coaches, English and journalism teachers, a print shop instructor and a Chicago newspaper critic. These memories are inspiring, compelling and, often, very moving. In one touching recollection, a teacher discouraged a young man from pursuing his career choice – a path he'd dreamed and prepared and practiced for years. Fortunately, that story had a happy ending. My goal is to have "My Teacher, My Future" encourage many more happy endings.

"My Teacher, My Future" is being distributed free of charge to every public middle school and high school, and private high school, and college and university in Indiana with a teacher training program. The book's publication and distribution is funded by a grant from the Educational Research Foundation of Indiana, Inc. The Foundation is a federally chartered 501(c)3 not-for-profit foundation with an almost 25-year history of awarding scholarships, book publishing, conducting educational workshops and seminars, and preparing research grants. Its activities are directed and monitored by an all-volunteer five-member board of directors.

That grant is funded by a bequest from the estate of James J. Krajewski, my son, a 1975 graduate of Munster High School in Munster, Indiana. Jim was an attorney who passed away too soon, and whom I believe may have been more fulfilled as a teacher.

Dr. Robert J. Krajewski, Ed.D.
Executive Director
Educational Research Foundation of Indiana, Inc.

TABLE OF CONTENTS

Charles J. Costa
Director, Northwest Indiana Education Service Center / 33

Steven Cramer
President, Bethel College / 35

Irv Cross
Executive Director, Big Brothers Big Sisters of Central Minnesota, former NFL Pro Bowler and CBS broadcaster / 36

E. Ronald Culp
Partner and managing director, Ketchum, Inc. / 38

Mitch Daniels
Governor of Indiana / 40

Jim Davis
Creator of "Garfield" / 42

Charlie DeMaio
Director of Development, Lambda Chi Alpha Educational Foundation / 44

John J. Doherty
Physical therapist / 45

Keary Dye
Administrator, Kindred Health Care / 46

John Ellis
Executive Director, Indiana Association of Public School Superintendents / 47

Daniel J. Elsener
President, Marian University / 49

Helen Engstrom
Director, Munster High School speech and debate program / 51

Dr. Harvey Feigenbaum
"The Father of Modern Echocardiography" / 53

John Flores
Former Superintendent of Schools, Maricopa, Arizona / 56

Bobby Fong
President, Butler University / 57

Adrianne, Chelsea and Meghan Francis
Students, Turkey Run High School / 59

Kenneth R.R. Gros Louis
Indiana University Chancellor and Trustee Professor / 61

Maria Halkias
Staff Writer, Dallas Morning News / 63

Frank Hanak
Retired teacher, principal, and school board member / 65

Mark A. Heckler
President, Valparaiso University / 66

Baron P. Hill
U.S. Representative, Indiana's Ninth District / 68

Edwin A. Hill
Vice President, Diversity –
Pharmaceutical Group Worldwide, Johnson & Johnson / 69

Mary Hill
2009 IHSAA Girls' Singles Tennis Champion / 70

Larry Hurt
1999 Indiana State Teacher of the Year / 71

Robin Jost
Owner, Tilles Interiors / 73

Dan Kadlec
Author and journalist / 75

Greg Kapp
Executive assistant to the president of Purdue University,
West Lafayette / 78

Theodore G. "Ted" Karras Sr.
1963 Chicago Bears World Championship Football Team / 79

Clyde Kersey
Indiana State Representative, District 43 / 81

Jeffrey J. Krajewski
Co-founder, Repairtime.com / 83

Karin Lee
Website developer and designer / 86

Norman Lowery
President and CEO, First Financial Bank,
and CEO, First Financial Corporation / 87

Richard Lugar
United States Senator / 88

Lloyd McClendon
Little League World Series record holder / 90

Edwin W. Miller
Chairman and CEO, Millennium Capital Group / 91

Spiro B. Mitsos
Retired co-founder, National Health Care Corp. / 92

Arden Moore
Author, radio talk show host and magazine editor / 93

Mark Morgan
Vice President, Business Planning and Administration,
Bayer Health Care / 96

James G. "Jay" Moseley
President, Franklin College / 97

John P. Newton
Vice President, Indiana State University Foundation / 98

Sandra Patterson-Randles
Chancellor, Indiana University Southeast, New Albany / 99

Mike Pettibone
Superintendent, Adams Central Community Schools / 101

Philip Potempa
Columnist, The Times of Northwest Indiana / 102

William Pullinsi
Artistic Director, Theatre at the Center / 104

Patrick Ralston
Former Director, Indiana Department of Natural Resources / 105

Dr. Gerald M. "Jerry" Reaven
Professor Emeritus, Stanford University / 106

Dennis Rittenmeyer
President, Calumet College of St. Joseph / 108

Amy Shojai
Author, certified animal behavior consultant / 111

Tavis Smiley
Broadcaster, author, advocate and philanthropist / 113

Quentin P. Smith
Member of the Tuskegee Airmen / 116

John P. Smyth
Former member, United States Olympic Committee,
and former director, USOC Olympic Training Centers / 118

Gayle Spiess
Software developer / 121

Albert "Al" Stevens
President and CEO, Opex Corporation / 123

Jack Stine
Retired COO, Northern Indiana Public Service Co. / 126

Sheryl Story
Attorney / 128

Mary Yorke
President, Munster School Board / 153

ANDREW J. ARNOLD

Founder and president, Precision Control Systems, Inc.

Andrew J. Arnold is living the dream. The business he founded nearly three decades ago now competes with industry giants – and he credits the technical writing skills that he learned from his high school journalism teacher for his success.

Howard Spangle supervised the student newspaper at Glenbard East High School in Lombard, Illinois. Mr. Spangle taught me how to write for effect -- to be more interesting and more concise by paying attention to column inches. I was the paper's sports editor and he pushed me to explore more than scores, statistics and results. While I pursued a career in engineering and sales, I always had an edge in technical writing that serves me to this day– and I attribute that edge to Mr. Spangle.

Andrew Arnold founded Precision Control Systems in Griffith in 1980. Since then, the firm has become one of the largest independently owned temperature control and energy retrofit providers in the Midwest. Arnold says that taking the firm from a start-up to a market leader against industry giants Honeywell, Siemens and Johnson Controls is his most treasured career accomplishment.

ALAN BARCUS

Author, composer, pianist, Masters Basketball player

If it weren't for a music teacher at LaPorte High School, no one would have ever heard the Car-X jingle, "Rattle, rattle, thunder, clatter, boom, boom, boom." That's because Alan Barcus, the composer who wrote the catchy tune, had no inkling of his musical gifts until his teacher encouraged him.

Gene Pennington, the head of instrumental music at LaPorte High School, pulled me aside when I was a sophomore and asked me if I realized I had musical abilities beyond that of the other orchestra members. I, of course, didn't believe it for a minute. He insisted on showing me how chord structures worked and sort of willed me into developing an interest in music.

Paul Selge, the varsity track coach at Indiana State University, did much the same thing. I had no experience as a runner, and he took me on as a project. For two years, he gave me instructions on diet, sleep, and the mental aspect of running, as well as the physical training.

Thanks to his track coach Paul Selge, Alan Barcus went on to set school records in five events at Indiana State University and was inducted into the school's Hall of Fame in 1997. He's also been honored as a Distinguished Alumni at ISU. He is currently a member of the Chicago Masters basketball team for men over 50, which won the national championship in 2001, 2002 and 2004. He's been the tournament MVP at the nationals twice.

He's also scored 11 movies, had six musicals and plays produced, and provided the music for some 2,400 television and radio commercials, including campaigns for McDonald's, Pepsi,

United Airlines and Kellogg's. But Barcus says: "The one everyone associates with me, and they might as well put this on the tombstone right now, is Car-X. 'Rattle, rattle, thunder, clatter, boom, boom, boom,' has been on the air for 26 years now."

LLOYD W. BENJAMIN III

Former President, Indiana State University

Acting, painting, classical music – the world of the arts opened up to Lloyd Benjamin thanks to a teacher. Benjamin says he headed off to college without any real focus, but a passion for the arts. To his great fortune, his freshman humanities teacher recognized that passion and nurtured it.

I recognize now that I was an eager learner as a college freshman, but unfocused and not well-disciplined academically. As the first in my family to go to college, I had no role models, but I was equipped with ample curiosity and a passion for reading and music, especially 19th century European.

Dr. Joseph Guillebeau, who taught Humanities at Emory-at-Oxford, recognized in me what I could not see for myself. He taught me to paint. He coaxed me to act in the Emory Players. He challenged me to be disciplined in expressing my feelings and ideas. He took me to my first-ever concert (Carmina Burana) and, most importantly, he confirmed and supported my interest in the arts which led to my finishing the bachelors in art history at Emory.

I have learned that I was the first Emory undergraduate to complete the Ph.D., in art history which I did at the University of North Carolina. I owe Dr. Guillebeau, and several other caring faculty members, a deep debt of gratitude.

Dr. Lloyd Benjamin says his most treasured career accomplishment was being named the tenth President of Indiana State University on July 1, 2000. Before that he served as vice president for academic affairs at Valdosta State University in Valdosta, Georgia, from 1995 to 2000. He was dean of the

College of Arts, Humanities, and Social Studies at the University of Arkansas at Little Rock from 1988 to 1995 and dean of the College of Fine Arts, UA-LR, from 1984 to 1988. He also served as acting dean of the College of Fine Arts and chair of the department of art, UA-LR, from 1983 to 1984.

Dr. Benjamin graduated from Emory University in 1966 with a B.A. in the history of art. In 1973, he earned his Ph.D. in art history from the University of North Carolina at Chapel Hill. He and his wife Wieke van der Weijden, who earned a Ph.D. in biochemistry from Leiden University, The Netherlands, have two grown children.

MARY BETH BONAVENTURA

Lake County Juvenile Court Judge

Fans of MTV's "Juvies" will remember Judge Mary Beth Bonaventura – she's the jurist who ruled the roost on the network's gritty documentary series. When first-time offenders walked into her courtroom in the Lake County Juvenile Center, many were literally shaking in their shoes. Their future was in her hands. What they didn't know is how a college psychology professor helped shape her decision-making as a judge.

Dr. Drew Appleby, my psychology professor at Marian College in Indianapolis, was always available before and after class to discuss school assignments or personal life issues. He was insightful and provoked ideas as to how life could be better or different, or why experiences held certain meaning in one's life. He expected excellence and inspired me to do the best I could. Dr. Appleby really began my interest in reaching out to folks who needed an attentive ear or shoulder to lean on.

I now refer to what I do as "I listen for a living" – which epitomizes the role of a judge: Listen and make decisions based on the law and what we hear and learn.

Mary Beth Bonaventura was named Senior Judge of the Lake Superior Court, Juvenile Division, in April 1993 after having served more than a decade as Magistrate in the Juvenile Court. She earned her undergraduate degree from Marian College and her law degree from Northern Illinois University in 1981. She worked as a Deputy Prosecutor in Lake County, and in 1982 began working in the Juvenile Court as a referee.

In 1986 Judge Bonaventura established and served as Executive Advisor for the Court Appointed Special Advocate

Program (CASA). Elected by her peers, the Judge served as Chief Judge of the Lake Superior Courts for the 1997-1999 term. She's been active on both the National and the Indiana Councils of Juvenile and Family Court Judges. In Lake County, she serves on the Boards of Directors for the American Red Cross, Lake County Mental Health Association, Southlake Mental Health Association and the Boys & Girls Clubs of Northwest Indiana.

Judge Bonaventura has received many prestigious awards during her career, and says her most treasured accomplishment has been mandating Lake County to build a new Juvenile Court and Detention Center.

VINCE BORYLA

1984 NBA Executive of the Year and 1948 Olympic gold
medalist

Vince Boryla admits that he was a "mediocre" basketball
player as a high school sophomore and junior. Then Nelson
"Doc" Irwin stepped in as the school's head coach – and taught
Boryla the fundamentals that transformed him into a competitive
first-string athlete, and eventually a successful businessman.

The most important teacher I ever had, who affected me
in so many ways, was Nelson "Doc" Irwin. During my senior
year, he came to East Chicago Washington High School as our
head basketball coach. He coached only one year, succeeding
Joe Pack who died unexpectedly.

Meeting "Doc" in September 1943 was a godsend for
me. I was a mediocre player on the basketball team during my
sophomore and junior years until he became our coach. "Doc"
spent many hours teaching me the dynamics and fundamentals of
basketball, which made me a more competitive player. We had a
very successful season and, in our sectional tournament, we
defeated Hammond Clark High School, which was ranked
number one in the state of Indiana. That evening we played in
the finals of the tournament and were defeated by Hammond
High, a team that we had easily defeated during the season. In
this game, I fouled out in the beginning of the fourth quarter, the
only game in which I fouled out in high school. I was really in
the "dumps" after that loss and it took me a long time to get over
it. However, with Doc's counsel, I worked my way through it
and received a scholarship to Notre Dame University. In my
second practice, I became the starting center and was a starter
throughout my basketball career.

I have often been asked about my accomplishments in
basketball and I have always given full credit to Doc Irwin. He

was years ahead of his time in his approach to coaching basketball and I always felt that I was privileged to have been under his tutelage.

His influence during those early years of high school basketball and the competitiveness that Doc instilled in me also allowed me to have a successful business career after my basketball career was over. I have always had the utmost respect for him and for his impact on my life.

As a freshman basketball player at the University of Notre Dame, Vince Boryla broke the school's scoring record and was named an All-American. He also played at the University of Denver, and was a member of the U.S. basketball team that won the gold medal at the 1948 Summer Olympics in London. Boryla played for the New York Knicks in the early 1950s, and coached the Knicks from 1956 to 1958.

He was the general manager of the American Basketball Association's Denver Nuggets early in their history and general manager of the ABA's Utah Stars. Boryla rejoined the Nuggets when the franchise joined the NBA and won the NBA Executive of the Year Award with the Nuggets in 1984. He's now retired and lives in Englewood, Colorado.

DR. OTIS R. BOWEN, M.D.

Physician and former Governor of Indiana

Father knows best. It may be a cliché, but Dr. Otis Bowen says it's true. His father's values and the example he set have guided Dr. Bowen throughout his life as a dedicated physician and one of Indiana's premier public servants.

My father Vernie Bowen began teaching at age 17 and taught all eight grades. He was also the janitor, and carried drinking water and wood to feed the wood-burning stove. After a few years he began teaching high school. He taught algebra, geometry, shop and mechanical drawing. In addition, he was the coach for boys' varsity basketball and baseball, as well as girls' basketball and seventh- and eighth-grade sports. Vernie was revered by his peers and his students. He was firm but fair.

He taught at schools in Kewanna, Fulton, Francesville, Crown Point and East Chicago. He retired, but soon began teaching again at the urging of the School Board. After five or six years he ended his teaching career after a total of 43 years.

Through the way he lived his life, my father taught me the value of honesty, hard work and thrift. These virtues have served me well throughout my lifetime. In addition to teaching, he was very involved in community service. His concern and care for others no doubt strongly influenced my decision to become involved in public service.

Dr. Otis Bowen served as Governor of Indiana from 1973 to 1981, and Secretary of Health and Human Services under President Ronald Reagan from 1985 to 1989. Before that, he served 14 years in the Indiana House of Representatives, including terms as Minority Leader, Majority Leader and Speaker of the House.

Dr. Bowen earned his medical degree from Indiana University in 1942, and in 1981 he took up the post of clinical professor of family medicine there. From 1943 to 1946 he served in the Medical Corps of the United States Army, rising from the rank of first lieutenant to captain. He has been awarded 30 honorary degrees.

Now 92, Dr. Bowen says his most treasured career accomplishment was shepherding the Medical Malpractice Act through the Indiana legislature. "The result was gaining more physicians to practice in Indiana and reversing the exiting of practicing physicians," said Dr. Bowen. "A companion piece of legislation created the EMS (Emergency Medical Service). Both have had a lasting impact on the citizens of Indiana."

MORGAN BURKE

Director of Athletics, Purdue University

Being treated as an adult – not a kid – by a high school history teacher at Brebeuf Jesuit Prep School in Indianapolis prepared Morgan Burke not just for college, but for life as well.

Fred McCashland, my sophomore U.S. history teacher, taught us to think and reason. Always prepared, always with energy, Fred could debate a point but never would he make us feel any different than a fellow adult. By treating us as adults, holding us to adult standards of preparedness, Fred prepared us for college and life thereafter. By the way, having a sense of humor was a real plus!

Morgan Burke is known as "the athletics director who came down from the grandstands" because he was an avid Purdue Boilermaker fan and member of the John Purdue Club long before he was appointed to lead Intercollegiate Athletics in 1992. A 1973 industrial management graduate and captain of the university's swim team as a senior, Burke was also a member of Phi Beta Kappa scholastic honorary society. He earned a master's degree in industrial relations at Purdue in 1975, and in 1980 he graduated with a law degree from John Marshall Law School in Chicago. He joined Inland Steel Co. after law school, moving through 13 positions in an 18-year span. He was vice president when he left to become Purdue's athletics director.

During Burke's tenure, the women's basketball team captured the 1999 national championship, the football team embarked on a run of 10 bowl games in 12 years from 1997 to 2008, and the men's basketball team achieved an unprecedented string of back-to-back-to-back Big Ten regular-season championships in 1994, 1995 and 1996.

STEPHEN CLINTON

President, Indiana Secondary Market for Education Loans, Inc.

A seventh-grade teacher who taught him how to focus and set goals was a game-changer for Stephen Clinton. Coming from a single-parent home, he needed that direction – and it gave him the self-confidence he needed to succeed in life.

Sister Eulalia – my seventh-grade teacher at St. Joseph's Elementary School in Kentland, Indiana -- was the first teacher who really influenced me and made me feel as though I had something to offer. She seemed to understand that I enjoyed reading and pushed me to read better literature and, more importantly, to try to understand the author's point of view. It was her belief in me that helped me to establish confidence in my own abilities if I focused and set goals. I took her inspiration and laid out life goals that have given me a sense of direction throughout my life. She was truly a life-changer for a boy from a single-parent household who badly needed some direction at that time in his life.

My second teacher was a professor at Indiana State University. While her name has vanished from my memory, I recall that she had a prior career as the editor of "Southern Living" magazine. She worked very closely with me to develop my writing skills. She led me to understand not only the art of communication but also the value of being able to convey your thoughts in an organized and precise way. I realized the value of her lessons when I saw how many well-educated people still struggle with written and spoken communication.

I probably cannot recall her name because it didn't seem important at the time, but as I established my career years later, it became clear that she had been a great teacher and inspiration to me.

Stephen Clinton graduated from Indiana State University in 1974 with a journalism degree, and went on to help others in their pursuit of higher education. He's served as president of Indiana Secondary Market for Education Loans, Inc., since 2002 and previously held the position from 1984 to 1992. Under his leadership, the organization has grown from $200 million in assets to over $1.5 billion and has generated 120 new jobs. In 2006 he was honored with ISU's Distinguished Alumni Award.

Clinton has also served as chairman of USA Group Secondary Market Services, Inc., a multibillion-dollar national financing organization for education loans. He also chaired USA Group Enterprises, Inc., Noel-Levitz Consulting Inc., and EDULINX Canada. He started his career at the U.S. Office of Education after graduating from ISU and later joined the Student Loan Marketing Association team, also known as Sallie Mae, in its beginnings.

He and his wife Bonnie reside in Fishers and have two children.

DR. JAMES COMER, M.D., M.P.H.

Associate Dean, Yale University School of Medicine,
and the Maurice Falk Professor of Child Psychiatry

Growing up, James Comer was one of five children in a low-income, African-American family. But his parents blessed their children with a great gift – the stability and support that enabled them to earn 13 college degrees between them.

His childhood convinced him that strong family support is key to educational success. Dr. Comer has built a career on that belief, and written extensively about education, child development and race relations.

Today Dr. Comer is one of American's leading social scientists, activists and educators. But looking back, he says it was a remark from his high school shop teacher that continues to guide him in everyday life.

I have had several favorite teachers, and many memorable experiences, during my lifetime. But one interaction in particular -- with Mr. Marvin Kincaid, my print shop teacher in 11th grade at East Chicago Washington High School -- has been an important touchstone throughout my life.

It's ironic that such an important and lifelong guide was obtained in print shop, where we used hand-held printing equipment that was eventually made obsolete by advances in technology. This experience speaks to the importance of teachers as thoughtful, reflective people in the lives of young people, regardless of what they teach.

I am not sure how or why the conversation took place, but Mr. Kincaid said to several of us, "You know, most of us will not make a contribution in life like that of Albert Einstein, Franklin D. Roosevelt, Joe Louis, or John D. Rockefeller. But we can all make an important contribution. We can all make important contributions by doing the best work that we can, taking care of ourselves and our family, and doing the best we can by our community and country."

Also, I was the sports editor for the school paper, and I drafted a story that would have been inflammatory. Mr. Kincaid didn't censor the story, but he did raise questions with me about how I thought different groups within the school would react to it. With his help, I thought about ways to address the issue that would be effective but not disruptive and polarizing. While this single incident did not do it all, I have operated in this way all of my life.

After graduating from Indiana University, James Comer earned his M.D. from Howard University and trained in psychiatry at Yale. He decided to specialize in psychiatry after observing the widespread depression and frustration among poor blacks in Washington's low-income areas.

Dr. Comer developed the School Development Program, often called the "Comer Process," at the Yale Child Study Center to help low-income children succeed in school. It's based on a simple principle: everyone with a stake in a school should have a say in how it's run.

His newest book is "Waiting for a Miracle: Why Schools Can't Solve Our Problems and How We Can." He has lectured widely across the United States and has served as a consultant to many projects, including the Children's Television Network.

NORMAN COMER

Retired Superintendent of Schools, East Chicago

A mathematics teacher who carved out extra time to help with his math problems – and also caught one of his football games – taught Norman Comer the value of a mentor.

My favorite teacher that encouraged me most was a mathematics teacher named Marie Brennecke. She was my advisor at East Chicago Washington High School from grades 7 through 12. She also was my geometry teacher in tenth grade. But, more than that, she was my mentor and a friend and was always there when I needed someone older and wiser to listen to me. On numerous occasions she made time on her lunch hour to delve more deeply into math problems beyond what I was learning in class.

She also went to one of my football games and thought the other players had killed me! She swore she'd never see another game. Yes, she was my favorite because I thought her concerns for me and my welfare were genuine and from the heart.

Like his brother Dr. James Comer, Norman Comer was born and raised in the Indiana Harbor section of East Chicago – and he says: "A more valuable experience I could never have profited from, even if I had to pay for it." A 1954 graduate of East Chicago Washington High School, he was third in his class of 254, an All-State halfback in football and president of the National Honor Society.

Dr. Comer says his most treasured career accomplishment was being named superintendent of schools in East Chicago in 1987 "after being told by a top-level administrator in 1960 that they couldn't even hire me as a black man in the high schools even though I had secondary teaching licenses in English and Social Studies from Northwestern University." He did get hired as an elementary school teacher and was later assigned to a high school. Dr. Comer recalls: "Although I was somewhat discouraged at the time, my mother - who had no formal education and worked as a domestic - was quite prophetic, assuring me, 'Some day you will be superintendent over there.' Proving once again, mother knows best!"

Now retired, Dr. Comer also served as executive dean at IVY Tech Community College.

CHARLES J. COSTA

Director, Northwest Indiana Education Service Center

"Hoosiers" isn't just a movie about Indiana basketball – it's a way of life. And while Charles Costa isn't a Hoosier born and bred, it was basketball that led him to his most memorable teacher – and a lesson that's guided him ever since.

I have lived and worked in Indiana for 30 years, but realize this is nowhere near long enough to qualify for true Hoosier status. Still, I'm honored to present a name for recognition in this publication. My exemplary teacher is actually someone I never had in class. Rather, he was my basketball coach and athletic director in high school. Larry Falloni was also a legend in Massachusetts high school basketball I would learn years later, winning three state basketball titles and retiring with a winning percentage of 71 percent.

I recall our basketball practices as extraordinarily organized – practically every second was scheduled and accounted for. I don't recall the practices as being lengthy at all, just very well run. There were no wasted moments. Designated times for individual skill development, team plays, offensive and defensive drills. One day I asked Coach Falloni how it was that he was so organized and successful. He responded, "I believe in the saying *'Luck is preparation meeting opportunity.'*" He went on to say that he believed preparation, which was anticipation combined with planning, was the key to success. Further, he hoped that his players would learn from his example.

He was right. Throughout my personal and professional life, I have tried to emulate what he modeled. And I have come to value more and more the wonderful lesson he taught me in the brief time that I had him as coach.

Dr. Charles Costa is director of the Northwest Indiana Education Service Center (NWIESC), a consortium of 24 public school corporations and private schools. He prepares its budget, annual plan and annual report. He also works with the NWIESC Natural Gas Cooperative, the Lake County Safe Schools Commission, and serves on the Board of Directors of the Northwest Indiana Challenger Learning Center. Dr. Costa also serves as the Executive Director of the Northwest Indiana Superintendent's Study Council.

Dr. Costa graduated from Providence College in 1967 with an A.B. in Political Science and served three years with the U.S. Peace Corps in varied educational assignments in Ethiopia. He met his wife Julie, a Peace Corps nursing volunteer there, and they were married by an Ethiopian prince at his palace.

He has an M.S. in Applied Linguistics and completed his doctorate in School Administration at Indiana University in 1984. He has served as an elementary and middle school principal, assistant superintendent and superintendent of schools.

STEVEN R. CRAMER

President, Bethel College

As a teenager, Steven Cramer was so badly injured in an accident that he wondered whether he even had a future. Then a teacher who also coached at his high school stepped in, and his mentoring put Cramer on the road to a career in education.

As a teenager I suffered a severe neck and spinal injury in a diving accident. During my recovery a coach and teacher at my high school, Mr. Long, went out of his way to visit me, encourage me and convince me that there was hope for my future. His encouragement and mentoring led me to pursue education as a career. This was reinforced when I was a college sophomore and the college's choir director, Dr. Tweed, pulled me aside to say that he saw potential for me as a music teacher. They both believed in me before I really believed in myself.

These two educators were great examples for me that great educators become "educational guides" and partners with students on their educational journey of discovery.

Steven R. Cramer was inaugurated in 2004 as the sixth president of Bethel College, an evangelical Christian college affiliated with the Missionary Church. He is a 1975 graduate of Bethel.

IRV CROSS

Executive Director, Big Brother Big Sisters of Central
Minnesota, former NFL Pro Bowler and CBS broadcaster

Today former National Football League players are all
over TV on "game day" – offering their analysis on pre-game,
post-game, and half-time shows. And every one of them owes a
debt to Irv Cross. A two-time Pro Bowler with the Philadelphia
Eagles, Cross was the first athlete to co-host the "NFL Today"
on CBS. Cross was awarded the 2009 Pete Rozelle Radio-
Television Award by the Pro Football Hall of Fame in
recognition of his broadcast accomplishments – and he credits
his fifth-grade teacher for jump-starting his broadcast career.

Ruth Ewing, my fifth-grade teacher at Maywood School
in Hammond, encouraged me to study for college. I was a shy
kid and one of 15 children. My mother died when I was in fifth
grade and Ruth Ewing provided the support and encouragement
to focus on my education. She even started a radio station in
class and made me managing editor. My grades improved, my
confidence grew and I ended up graduating from Northwestern
University and working for the CBS-TV network for 23 years on
the "NFL Today." It was the highest-rated sports studio show for
17 years, and I received the Pete Rozelle Award in recognition of
my broadcasting career.

Irv Cross is now executive director of the Big Brothers
Big Sisters of Central Minnesota. He spent 23 years with CBS
Sports as a studio host and game analyst. He appeared on the
"NFL Today" from its inception in 1975 until 1989. The first
African-American to anchor a network sports show, he co-

anchored with Brent Musberger, Phyllis George and Jimmy "The Greek" Snyder.

Cross was special assistant to the president of Macalaster (Minnesota) College for development and was also director of athletics until May 2006. He served as athletic director of Idaho State University from 1996 to 1998.

He played football at Northwestern University under Coach Ara Parseghian, and was captain of the 1960 team as well as an All-Big Ten pick. Cross was a seventh-round draft pick of the Philadelphia Eagles in 1963, and was also drafted by the New York Titans of the American Football League and the Toronto Argonauts of the Canadian Football League. He played 10 seasons with the Eagles and the Los Angeles Rams, making the Pro Bowl twice.

He and his wife Liz live in the Twin Cities. They have a son Matt and daughter Sarah.

E. RONALD CULP

Partner and managing director, Ketchum, Inc.

Grammar, grammar and more grammar! The lessons that Ron Culp learned from his English teacher at Remington High School – where there were only 41 students in his graduating class in 1965 -- laid the groundwork for a stand-out career in public relations.

Never end a sentence with a preposition!

Seldom does a day go by that I don't recall that grammar rule or several more that Mrs. Miller made come to life in my tenth-, eleventh- and twelfth-grade English class at Remington High School. She was one of those special teachers who made English fun, while making sure we understood the importance of English to our future success.

Mrs. Miller also directed school plays, and the students in her English classes were the first to volunteer since she made those experiences fun as well. She always greeted every class with a smile and was able to be stern without being unreasonable. She still comes to most class reunions and school events although she's been retired for many years. And she still smiles and proudly reminds us of things that we did during our high school days.

Those high school English classes provided the foundation for my 40-year career in communications at four Fortune 500 corporations – Eli Lilly, Pitney Bowes, Sara Lee and Sears.

But Mrs. Miller was not alone in her personalized impact on students lucky enough to attend Remington High School. Others included language teacher Florence Bowman, who taught me Latin. Even though I hated the class at the time, I liked her and later realized that I learned about our own language through studying Latin . . . and I now wish I had studied even harder in her class.

Marilee Goad was the most amazing business education/typing teacher. We learned on manual upright typewriters and I still hit the keys on my computer with the same force that I did that old Royal machine. I reached 110 words per minute with fewer than three errors, and I'm even faster today thanks to computer keyboards. But I think of Mrs. Goad often as I marvel at my own typing skills!

A retired Senior Vice President of Public Relations and Government Affairs at Sears, Roebuck and Co., Ron Culp is now a partner and managing director at Ketchum, Inc., a global public relations firm. "My blog –www.culpwrit.com– provides guidance to young people pursuing careers in public relations," said Mr. Culp, who currently serves on the boards of the Economic Club of Chicago, the Lincoln Park Zoo, Gilda's Club, the Plank Center for Leadership in Public Relations, and the Chicagoland Chamber of Commerce.

MITCH DANIELS

Governor of Indiana

"Heckle training." That's what Governor Mitch Daniels calls the lessons he learned from his no-nonsense ninth-grade English teacher Nina Heckle – and her strict standards not only elevated his academic performance and sharpened his skills, but have made him a tough taskmaster for his staff members over the years.

I've always believed that the teachers we remember the most fondly are those of whom we were not that fond at the time, those teachers who pushed us the hardest and were the most unbending in their insistence that we learn our lessons fully and do our very best.

Nina Heckle was that sort of teacher. If someone in Hollywood had called Central Casting and requested a candidate to play a severe, demanding, no-nonsense ninth-grade English teacher, they'd have sent over someone who looked and acted like Mrs. Heckle.

It was futile to try to slip a fragment of clumsy syntax past her, to say nothing of a grammatical error, a punctuation mistake, or (heaven forbid!) a misspelled word. Her students were required to read a lot and write a lot, and papers that fell short of her standards came back again and again until they were satisfactory. She must have had a sense of humor, but at least in my memory she left it at the classroom door. Once the bell rang she was all business, and therefore so were we.

In all the years since, I have had occasion to use my Heckle training in writing millions of words, and also in correcting the work of hundreds of beleaguered staff members, who probably have chafed under my unreasonable standards as we once complained about Nina's. I hope that my victims have concluded in retrospect that the extra work and irritation were more than offset by improvement in the essential life skills of communication and exposition.

Nina Heckle never wasted her time or ours trying to artificially elevate our "self-esteem." Instead, she elevated our academic performance and readiness for the world that awaited us, and because of her, when we reached that world, self-esteem came naturally.

Mitch Daniels was elected to his second term as Indiana's 49th Governor in November 2008. He also served as Director of the Office of Management and Budget under President George W. Bush and worked for Eli Lilly and Company.

When he graduated from North Central High School in 1967, Daniels was named Indiana's Presidential Scholar by President Lyndon B. Johnson. He earned a bachelor's degree from Princeton University in 1971 and graduated from Georgetown University Law Center in 1979.

Daniels served as U.S. Senator Richard Lugar's chief of staff during his first term from 1977 to 1982, and managed three successful Senate campaigns for Lugar.

In 2008, Governor Daniels started the Hoosier High School Math and Science Awards, naming a Mister/Miss Math and Science, similar to the state's Mr. Basketball, to recognize the state's best high school students in math and science.

JIM DAVIS

Creator of "Garfield"

An art teacher with an eye for talent made sure that a budding cartoonist got the time – and attention – he needed to develop his skills. That budding cartoonist, Jim Davis, went on to create "Garfield" the cat. Perhaps not surprisingly, he's still in touch with his favorite teacher Paull McCoy -- his art teacher for four years at Fairmount High School.

Paull McCoy was an artist's artist. He sported a flat-top and a goatee. He was a talented musician. He played trumpet for Tommy Dorsey. Scratch Paul and you'd find a beatnik.

Paull pushed me for four years in high school, never quite satisfied with my output. He said he wouldn't have been so tough on me if I weren't so good. My senior year I had a scheduling conflict for art. So, he gave me the art room to myself for an hour each day. Once a week, we met before school for a review of my week's output. As gruff as he was, I knew he believed in me.

Paull's in his 90s now. I gave him a tour of the studio recently. He no longer has the flat-top. He has a pony-tail.

Jim Davis grew up on a small farm in Fairmount and graduated from Fairmount High School. He attended Ball State University and says his most treasured career accomplishments are creating the comic strip "Garfield," and the day the strip was syndicated in 1978. Today "Garfield" is syndicated in about 2,400 newspapers and is read by an estimated 250 million fans each day.

Davis has written Emmy Award-winning TV specials and was also a producer on the "Garfield & Friends" TV series that aired on CBS from 1988 to 1995. He is the writer and co-producer of an anticipated trilogy of CGI-direct-to-video feature films about Garfield. The first, "Garfield Gets Real," was released in 2007.

Davis and his family live in Albany. He works out of a studio there, overseeing the "Garfield" empire with staff members of his firm Paws, Inc. He recently founded the Professor Garfield Foundation to support children's literacy.

CHARLIE DeMAIO

Director of Development, Lambda Chi Alpha Educational Foundation

Every child learns the lesson that "It's better to give than to receive." But a college professor taught the true value of that lesson to Charlie DeMaio.

I became a volunteer for Indiana State University's School of Technology. My company eventually sponsored two scholarships and donated much-needed equipment.

I brought in guest speakers and taught as a guest lecturer. What I learned is that giving back is more important than receiving recognition. Dr. Robert Cooksey, director of ISU's packaging program, taught me the value of giving.

Charlie DeMaio is a 1973 graduate of Indiana State University, and has received the school's Distinguished Service Award and William Albert Jones Award. He also is a past president of the Indiana State Alumni Board of Directors.

As director of development for Lambda Chi Alpha Educational Foundation, he has responsibilities for planned giving, major gifts, and estate planning. Previously, he held positions within the packaging industry for 30 years, including vice president of sales, division manager, and national accounts manager.

JOHN J. DOHERTY

Physical therapist

In college football, winning the national championship is the ultimate crowning glory. And if not for his high school religion teacher, John Doherty would not have been a proud member of the Fighting Irish team that won the national football championship in 1977.

I was ready to quit as a student manager/athletic trainer my sophomore or junior year in high school. But Brother Linus – the freshman football coach and my ninth-grade religion teacher at St. John's Prep in Danvers, Massachusetts – talked me out of it. Had he not, I would not have pursued the career that I did. He had the unique ability to mix humor with serious lessons in the classroom and on the field. Whenever I give a lecture at a career-day event, I bring my memories of Brother Linus into the classroom.

John J. Doherty was the student and staff athletic trainer of the University of Notre Dame's varsity football team from 1977 to 1981. He has been the head athletic trainer at Munster High School since 1985, and was the trainer for their state championship varsity baseball team in 2002. He is self-employed as a physical therapist and writes a weekly sports medicine column for The Times of Northwest Indiana.

KEARY DYE

Administrator, Kindred Health Care

"Believe in yourself!" The professor who communicated that simple lesson gave Keary Dye the confidence to succeed in college.

Dr. James Misenheimer, my freshman writing instructor at Indiana State University, taught me to believe in myself – and that I had the tools to be successful in college if I was willing to work hard. He taught me the value of being well-read and to broaden my horizons by reading great literature.

Keary Dye is an administrator with Kindred Health Care at the Columbus (Indiana) Health and Rehabilitation Center. In 2006 he was named Executive Director of the Year for Kindred Health Care for the Central Indiana District while at the Southwood Health and Rehabilitation Center in Terre Haute. Dye was also assistant executive director of Regency Place of Greenwood. He has served on the Hendricks County United Way Community Solutions Board.

Dye is a life member of the Indiana State University Alumni Association. He and his wife Simone live with their son Evan in Avon.

02/11/11

JOHN ELLIS

Executive Director, Indiana Association of Public School Superintendents

When you're a teacher, your working day doesn't end when the last bell rings. John Ellis is still touched by the compassion of the teacher who reached out to him when he was a frightened 7-year-old.

I need to thank many teachers, but I have chosen two that had the greatest impact on my life. My second grade teacher Mrs. Grogg (I was 15 before I discovered that teachers had first names) called me *at home* every night my mother was in the hospital for cancer surgery. She didn't allow that seven-year-old boy to withdraw into himself to handle a frightening and confusing time alone.

In high school, my speech teacher John Roscoe (I was 15 and knew his first name) forced me out of a shell I had constructed during my middle school years. Mr. Roscoe taught me to step forward and express my own opinions. Those who know me well may hold him responsible for this development. He also taught me I had better be able to back up my opinions with facts. He thought it was great to show a sense of humor and even encouraged expressing humor in his classroom. He talked to us, rarely at us.

A Chinese proverb states: "A child's life is like a piece of paper on which every passerby leaves a mark." From one teacher to many others, past and present, thanks for the marks you have made.

Dr. John Ellis attended J.E. Ober Elementary School in Garrett, graduated from Garrett High School and earned degrees from Ball State and Indiana State universities. Before becoming executive director of the Indiana Association of Public School Superintendents, he was superintendent of the Jennings County schools for eight years and the Noblesville schools for 12 years. He says his most treasured career accomplishment has been leading a change in district writing practices that resulted in a substantial increase in students' writing scores.

DANIEL J. ELSENER

President, Marian University

Politicians sometimes get a bad rap. But a state legislator who was also his college professor took Daniel Elsener under his wing – and showed him that teachers can make a difference.

Perhaps the most memorable break I got in my career came from another educator. While attending a small liberal arts college in Nebraska, I met a man who would influence my future in ways I wouldn't recognize until many years later.

Nebraska state senator Richard Marvel was also my college professor and mentor, and he took an interest in my success that stays with me to this day. Sen. Marvel was the first person to encourage me to be a teacher. He introduced me to amazing opportunities – from teaching civil liberties at a penitentiary to conducting research for political campaigns. He was the first person to give me an opportunity to use my mind, more than physicality, to earn a wage.

I remember doing research for a political campaign – a job he helped me secure. I was having a difficult time trying to organize what I had found and present it in a compelling way. Sen. Marvel told me to come to his home one weekend and he'd help me organize the research. I remember being sort of dumbfounded that he would take the time and invite me to his home. This was a very important lawmaker – someone who had many people to see and many things to do. And yet he wanted to make a personal investment of time to help me.

We laid all of the research notes out on the dining room table, and he walked me through what needed to be done and helped me focus. To this day I am amazed at the time he gave to me. He never acted too important for me. He was generous with his time and his wisdom. That generosity has stayed with me and grounded me.

Sen. Marvel taught me the value of mentoring and teaching. I see that same spirit in the professors and staff at Marian University. It is intense, it is personal, and it is relevant to our students. Sen. Marvel encouraged me and showed me that teachers can make a difference and active learning is the key to success. That's why I'm dedicated to providing the same opportunities to today's students and tomorrow's teachers.

Sen. Marvel's philosophy has now become my own: People will rise to your expectations of them. If you treat them as if they are smart and talented, and engage them in important endeavors, they will begin to view themselves as effective and significant.

Daniel J. Elsener became president of Marian College, now Marian University, on August 1, 2001. He holds a bachelor's degree in political science from Nebraska Wesleyan University and a master's degree in education administration from the University of Nebraska.

His journey includes service as a teacher in Omaha, Nebraska; high school principal in Topeka, Kansas; and superintendent of Catholic schools for the Diocese of Wichita, Kansas. He served the Archdiocese of Indianapolis as secretary/executive director in the Office of Catholic Education and then as secretary/executive director for the Office of Stewardship and Development.

HELEN ENGSTROM

Director, Munster High School speech and debate program

Mentors are as key to teachers as they are to people in the business world – and Helen Engstrom's mentor helped her to shape the skills of countless high school students.

When I first started the speech and debate team at Munster High School, my mentor was a legendary coach from Jefferson High School in Lafayette, Indiana. James Hawker coached awesome teams and was later the president of the National Forensic League. The National Forensic League's purpose is to encourage and motivate high school students to participate in and become proficient in the forensic arts: debate, public speaking, and interpretation.

By watching Mr. Hawker's students perform and listening to his keen advice, I was able to build and direct a program at Munster that has produced scores of successful young speakers who have learned marketable skills to serve them in their adult lives. Without a mentor like him, I likely would never have directed the successful program at Munster, which has grown from 13 students to 250 students annually. Nor would I have had the privilege of working with the program's outstanding coaches.

Helen Engstrom has been the director of Munster High School's speech and debate program for 44 years. Although she retired in 1995 from teaching English and speech, she continues to direct the speech and debate program four days a week, and recently received the prestigious "fifth diamond" from the National Forensic League. A minimum of 25 years of coaching and 130,000 credit points amassed by student team members are required for the honor. She says her most treasured career accomplishment is "teaching young people the marketable skills of communication" and being selected to the National Forensic League's Coaching Hall of Fame.

DR. HARVEY FEIGENBAUM, M.D.

"The Father of Modern Echocardiography"

The violin was Harvey Feigenbaum's first love. But when the symphony orchestra director at his high school steered him away from playing the instrument professionally, Feigenbaum followed his advice. He studied pre-med instead and went on to do groundbreaking research that's saved countless lives. Dr. Feigenbaum has no regrets about the path he chose, he says, but nearly 50 years later, he still remembers the last time he played the violin.

Neither of my parents graduated from high school. My father had the equivalent of an eighth-grade education in his native Poland, but despite his lack of formal education he was fluent in at least seven different languages. And being a merchant in the Indiana Harbor section of East Chicago, he used all seven languages regularly. My mother was raised in Chicago, and while she attended high school, I don't think she graduated. This lack of education must have been a powerful incentive to see that their children would have the best education available. As a result, both my sister Lorraine and I graduated high school and college. I also went to medical school.

My parents had another love besides education, and that was music. They saw to it that both Lorraine and I played musical instruments. Lorraine took piano lessons and majored in piano in college. She still plays the piano today. I played the violin, and this leads me to the teacher who had the greatest impact in my life – Charles Buckley, the director of the East Chicago Washington High School symphony orchestra. He actually lived in Chicago, Illinois, and was the music critic for the Chicago Herald American newspaper. But he traveled to East Chicago every day because he loved working with young musicians. Mr. Buckley worked with my sister Lorraine first. By the time she was in high school, Lorraine had already been playing the piano for some time. She also took up the viola in high school and played it in the orchestra. Mr. Buckley recognized her piano abilities and had her playing the piano in the orchestra as often as possible. Mr. Buckley met my parents and became a close friend of our family.

When I entered high school I had been playing the violin for several years and immediately entered the orchestra. By my junior year I was the concert master. I played at school events as a member of the orchestra, as a soloist and with small groups on many occasions. Playing the violin was a major part of my life. When I was nearing graduation in 1951, I went to Mr. Buckley and asked him to help me decide what to do with my life and what role the violin would play.

Mr. Buckley sat down with me and described the professional life of a musician and what future he thought I might have. He "gave it to me straight." He felt that my chances of being a successful soloist were next to nil. My most likely prospect was as a symphony orchestra player. Since I also had an interest in science, he strongly recommended that pursuing some scientific endeavor would be a much better opportunity for me.

I took his advice. At Indiana University I took mostly science courses and eventually became pre-med. But I still couldn't stop playing the violin. I rented a practice room in the music school and continued to practice every day as I had been doing since I was eight years old. I also sat in with the Indiana University orchestra periodically. This routine lasted for about two years. Mr. Buckley was right. I never would have been a successful soloist, and I don't believe I would be happy as a violinist in a symphony orchestra.

I stopped playing violin for at least a year. When I was accepted to medical school, I decided to surprise my parents and arranged for a piano-playing fraternity brother to accompany me in performing at the fraternity parents' day affair just prior to my starting medical school. My parents were surprised and very pleased to say the least. That was the last time I ever played the violin.

Dr. Harvey Feigenbaum is a distinguished professor of medicine at the Indiana University School of Medicine and director of the echocardiography laboratories at Indiana University Hospital.

He graduated with honors from Indiana University undergraduate and medical schools. Intrigued by a 1963 ad claiming that ultrasound could measure cardiac volume, he eventually developed the world's first practical, popular use of echocardiography using cardiac ultrasound to detect pericardial effusion. His laboratory subsequently developed many more applications. He trained many early pioneers in echocardiography and the first cardiac sonographers.

Dr. Feigenbaum is the founding editor of the "Journal of the American Society of Echocardiography" and is on the editorial board of numerous other medical journals. He is a Fellow of the American College of Physicians, American College of Cardiology and the Council of Clinical Cardiology, American Heart Association. He is also Founder and Past President of the American Society of Echocardiography.

A member of Phi Beta Kappa, he has been recognized with numerous honors, including the Primio Mantevergine Award as "Father of Modern Echocardiography" in Naples, Italy, in June 2004. He is also the recipient of the Pioneer Award from Mayo Clinic for Development of Echocardiography at a 50th celebration meeting. He was awarded the 2005 Living Legend Award from the Indiana Historical Society, the American Heart Association Distinguished Scientist award in November 2005, and named International Honorary Member, Japanese College of Cardiology in September 2006.

JOHN FLORES

Former Superintendent of Schools, Maricopa, Arizona

For John Flores and his classmates, failure was not an option in the classes taught by two remarkable high school teachers.

Grace Nestbit, an English teacher at East Chicago Roosevelt High School, cared about her students very much. Both she and Mrs. Diane Sarkotich, an English literature teacher at Roosevelt, would not allow us to fail. Both of them motivated, encouraged and evaluated us until we succeeded. They cared about their students and the impact they had on us was positive.

Formerly the superintendent of schools in Maricopa, Arizona, Flores says his most treasured career accomplishment was being principal of Maine West High School in 1997, when it was ranked 16th in the country by U.S. News and World Report.

BOBBY FONG

President, Butler University

Even in elementary school, Bobby Fong learned lessons in teaching, scholarship and administration from his favorite teacher – and when she retired, an entire neighborhood honored her.

Mrs. Marjorie Davis – a fifth- and sixth-grade teacher at Lincoln Elementary School in Oakland, California – was legendary among a cadre of teachers who guided a generation of Chinese immigrant children into the American mainstream. They taught us English as a second language and encouraged our academic inspirations.

Mrs. Davis developed a system whereby students who finished an assignment first would turn and tutor classmates who were having difficulty. The tutors actually facilitated their own learning because there's no better way to master a subject than to teach it to another.

She was also the sponsor of the school traffic squad, which had especial cachet. I was captain of the squad in sixth grade, and the responsibility included organizing fellow students and creating schedules. It was my first leadership experience.

Mrs. Davis shaped me for teaching, scholarship and administration. When she retired, all of Chinatown threw a banquet in her honor.

Dr. Bobby Fong became the 20th president of Butler University on June 1, 2001. The first American-born child of Chinese immigrants, he grew up in Chinatown in Oakland, California. His father was a butcher and his mother a seamstress in a sweatshop.

He was elected to Phi Beta Kappa at Harvard University, and graduated with an A.B. in English in 1973. Fong earned his doctorate in English literature from UCLA in 1978, and began his academic career at Berea College in Kentucky, where he taught from 1978 to 1989. He became professor of English and dean for arts and humanities at Hope College in Holland, Michigan, in 1989, then accepted a position as dean of the faculty and professor of English at Hamilton College in Clinton, New York, in 1995.

Dr. Fong is a fan of the New York Yankees, and an avid baseball card collector.

A scholar of the 19th century Irish writer Oscar Wilde, Dr. Fong says his most treasured career accomplishment is acting as editor of "Poems and Poems in Prose," volume one in "The Complete Works of Oscar Wilde," published by the Oxford University Press. The book was named "Choice Outstanding Academic Book of 2001."

ADRIANNE, CHELSEA and MEGHAN FRANCIS

Students, Turkey Run High School

The Francis triplets have transformed the girls' basketball team at Turkey Run High School into a force to be reckoned with. The sisters look nothing alike, but on the floor they connect like a dynamic trio. Adrianne averaged 10 points and eight rebounds per game in her freshman season, while Chelsea is the team's starting guard and Meghan dresses for both junior varsity and varsity. Their coach Sam Karr says: "I couldn't find three better kids to coach. They are model student athletes."

ADRIANNE
There are many teachers that I've liked during the years I've been in school. The one who stands out the most is Susan Seitz. She is like me in many ways. She is outgoing and makes her classes fun. Ms. Seitz also acknowledges that I am my own person, not just a Francis triplet. Ms. Seitz is not just a teacher, but a friend. She is there for you if you need help. She also cares about each student she's taught.

Allison Whitman was my ninth-grade English teacher. She told me that even though I love sports, I still need to focus on education because education is the key to life. There is a possibility that you could get hurt playing a sport so you need a good, solid education to fall back on if something like that does happen.

CHELSEA
I was Ms. Beth Duley's staff assistant my sophomore year. Whatever she asked me to do, I did it. One day when the seniors were working on a project, Ms. Duley and I started talking. She said to me, "Don't let anyone change you. Be yourself." Ever since that day, I have been myself. I haven't changed so someone would like me.

MEGHAN

Mr. Joey Hart, my freshman geometry teacher, quickly became Coach Hart during my basketball season. He is my school's Athletic Director, Boys' Varsity Basketball Coach, and geometry teacher. Whenever I was in his class, we'd sit and talk about basketball. After the season was over, I went to my sisters' sports banquet. They both got all-conference that year. Coach Hart leaned over to me and said, "Meghan, are you always going to sit on the sidelines and play cheerleader, or are you going to work on your game and play with your sisters next year? Maybe next year you won't come to this banquet as a guest." After that banquet, I stayed after school every day and played 3-on-3 with the varsity boys who didn't play baseball. My hard work and determination fueled by those two sentences at the banquet paid off. I wasn't a varsity starter yet, and I didn't make all-conference, but I lettered in basketball my sophomore year.

The Francis triplets were born in Indianapolis and are being raised in Bloomingdale where they attend Turkey Run High School. Besides their stand-out play on the basketball court, they also share a unique bond at home, often assisting their parents Karen and Larry with the caring of foster children.

KENNETH R.R. GROS LOUIS

Indiana University Chancellor and Trustee Professor

The famed literary critic Lionel Trilling had the unique gift of making characters come to life – a talent that Kenneth R.R. Gros Louis tried to emulate in his own lectures.

Lionel Trilling was one of the distinguished literary critics and minds of the 20th century. He and a colleague at Harvard fought for years to teach a course on contemporary literature, but were often blocked because the argument was made that the authors to be read might not "survive" into the future. They finally got approval to teach such a course shortly after World War 2.

I enrolled in Trilling's year-long course as a sophomore at Columbia College in New York City. It was stunning. What struck me most was a cab ride that he and I shared accidentally in which he described to me the great difficulty of teaching the course. "What I'm really doing, you know," he said, "is teaching about myself and my generation. It's not just Hemingway or Kafka or Mann or Proust, etc., but it's about me and therefore intensely personal."

Trilling predicted in an essay written in the 1950s that the teaching of contemporary literature, with its criticism of American values, could quite likely lead to a rebellion 10 or 20 years beyond the 1950s. How prophetic he was.

His lectures were extraordinarily stimulating and he always could make characters come to life by describing them as if they were in Central Park or on campus or talking with us in one of our dorm rooms. I admired that gift and have tried to emulate it.

Kenneth R.R. Gros Louis was named Trustee Professor at Indiana University in 2001 after retiring as Vice President for Academic Affairs and Bloomington Chancellor. He returned in 2004 as Senior Vice President for Academic Affairs and Bloomington Chancellor. He was named University Chancellor in 2006.

Chancellor Gros Louis received B.A. and M.A. degrees from Columbia University and his Ph.D. in Medieval and Renaissance Literature from the University of Wisconsin. He joined IU in 1964 as a faculty member in the departments of English and Comparative Literature. Over the years he served as acting chair of Comparative Literature, chair of the Department of English, associate dean of the College of Arts and Sciences, and Dean of the College. In 1980 he was named Vice President for the Bloomington campus. In 1988 he was named Vice President of Academic Affairs and Bloomington campus Chancellor.

MARIA HALKIAS

Staff Writer, Dallas Morning News

A high school journalism teacher singled her out for an award and a college journalism professor nicknamed her "Turkey" – and that "special" attention fostered Maria Halkias' interest in a newspaper career.

Robert Draba was one of the English teachers at Lew Wallace High School in Gary in the early 1970s. He was in charge of the Philosopher newspaper and the Quill and Blade yearbook.

Mr. Draba and principal Christ Christoff believed in a free press and let us tackle topics from a new dress code and hall pass rules to the Vietnam War and a hateful radio broadcaster who spewed lies about our school's safety on a local radio station. (The FCC eventually took action against him.)

Mr. Draba made a decision my senior year that had a lot to do with my pursuing a career in journalism. Each year, The Gary Post-Tribune would give out its "Most Valuable Staffer Award." At our school it alternated between a staffer on the newspaper and the yearbook. My senior year it was the yearbook's turn, so as a newspaper staffer, I didn't even wonder. But I received the award. Mr. Draba, I still have the plaque.

I enrolled at Valparaiso University as a business major in 1973. There I met journalism professor Carl Galow who helped me switch majors and put together an interdisciplinary program for me.

Professor Galow called me -- and probably a few others that I didn't know about – "Turkey." Sounds silly, but it made me feel special. My senior year he gave me what he said was the best internship he had, a stint at the LaPorte Herald Argus. (Newspaper internships were rare back then.) It was several miles away driving in some wicked snow storms. I would get back to the campus with my stomach in knots, but with a little more validation that this was how I wanted to make a living. Thank you, Professor Galow.

Maria Halkias graduated from Gary's Lew Wallace High School in 1973 and Valparaiso University in 1977. She has reported for newspapers in Gary and Jackson, Mississippi. She is currently a staff writer with the Dallas Morning News.

FRANK HANAK

Retired teacher, principal and school board member

A teacher who made him "comfortable" in math class – not his favorite subject – inspired Frank Hanak to consider teaching as a career.

Mathematics wasn't my favorite subject. Oh, I got by, but I was always fearful of making a mistake until I had Mrs. Florence Johnson for math in the eighth grade. Maybe it was her kindly personality, or her soft voice never berating me for a wrong answer, but I was finally comfortable in a math class.

I had an inkling at that time that I wanted to be a teacher. If that ever came to pass, I thought that I'd try to have a classroom where the students would be as "comfortable" as Mrs. Johnson made me.

A 1938 graduate of East Chicago Washington High School, Frank Hanak went on to work on the Inland Steel ore boats and in the Number 2 open hearth before Army service in World War 2. The GI bill enabled him to become a teacher. He taught fifth grade in the Griffith schools and retired as an elementary school principal in 1987. He went on to serve on the Griffith School Board for eight years.

Hanak is co-founder of Washington High's alumni association and editor of its monthly newsletter, The Anvil. That was the name of the school's weekly newspaper, an apt title for a school located in what was once the very heart of America's steel production. The newsletter is funded by voluntary contributions from nearly 1,300 alums scattered across the continental United States, plus Hawaii, Vancouver, Canada, and even Australia.

MARK A. HECKLER

President, Valparaiso University

"The Music Man" was a smash hit on Broadway way back in 1957. But even today mentioning a certain Hoosier city often prompts people to break into the show's most catchy tune "Gary, Indiana." And while the famous musical was set in River City, Iowa, it could just as easily have been set in Windber, Pennsylvania, the small coal-mining town where Mark Heckler's own personal "music man" set him on his life's path.

Louis Guisto was an impresario in our tiny community. He was a larger-than-life figure, filled with boisterous energy, always wearing a big smile, always surrounded by people eager to talk with him. He was many things in our small town -- from businessman to mayor -- but, most importantly, he was my music teacher and band director.

Mr. Guisto instilled in me a love for music that continues to this day. His attention and encouragement helped to grow my self-esteem during those awkward adolescent years. And when he left our small town after many years, both young and old knew that our community had lost an important part of its soul.

That's the thing about great teachers--they inspire us, they lead us, they energize us. Yet, all too often, we take them for granted. And when they leave, a school and a community may never be the same again.

Mark A. Heckler is the 18th president of Valparaiso University. Previously, he was provost and vice chancellor for academic and student affairs at University of Colorado-Denver. He joined the staff there in 1995 as a tenured professor of theatre and director of the School of Arts. Before that, he was director of theatre and professor of fine arts at New York's Siena College for 16 years. While in New York, he was also managing director of an outdoor summer professional theatre for two years. His artistic career as an actor, director and designer comprises more than 100 academic and professional productions in the United States, Europe and the Middle East.

He earned a B.A. in communications with honors from Pennsylvania's Elizabethtown College in 1977, and a Master of Fine Arts in drama from Catholic University in Washington, D.C., in 1979. He and his wife Veronica have four children.

BARON P. HILL

U.S. Representative, Indiana's Ninth District

Baron Hill -- whose wife Betty recently retired from teaching math and social studies at Seymour Middle School – says: "As the husband of a public schoolteacher, I strongly believe that our schools are where opportunities for the future shine the brightest. As a Member of Congress, I believe that all necessary resources must be provided to state and local governments in order to secure that future."

My second-grade teacher Mrs. Dinsmore always served as a vivid inspiration to me during my educational years in Seymour. She was a wonderful teacher.

Baron Hill was born and raised in Seymour, and is a member of the Indiana Basketball Hall of Fame. He served in the Indiana House of Representatives from 1982 to 1990, and served as the U.S. Representative from Indiana's Ninth District from 1999 to 2005, and 2007 to present.

EDWIN A. HILL

Vice President, Diversity – Pharmaceutical Group Worldwide,
Johnson & Johnson

When his high school French teacher applied her own special "treatment," Ed Hill realized that she truly cared.

Mrs. Elizabeth Williamson was my French teacher at Gary Roosevelt High School. She worked hard at encouraging every student to pronounce words in FRENCH accurately by applying her own special "TREATMENT."

This "treatment" involved a light symbolic "choking" by placing her hands on our shoulders and giving us a gentle "shaking" as she emphasized the correct pronunciation. This "treatment" and her "touch" showed me that SHE CARED!!!

Ed Hill is a 1969 graduate of Gary Roosevelt High School and a 1973 graduate of Indiana State University with a B.S degree. In 2003 the university honored him as a Distinguished Alumni. Hill served as a placement consultant at ISU until 1975 when he accepted a position with RCA Records/Consumer Electronics in Indianapolis, and in 1988 he joined the Johnson & Johnson Family of Companies as the manager of employee relations. In 2004 he was promoted to Vice President, Diversity – Pharmaceutical Group Worldwide for Johnson & Johnson in Brunswick, New Jersey.

Since recovering from multiple myeloma in 1988, he has been active in support of the Multiple Myeloma Research Foundation along with other charities. His wife Brenda, a registered nurse, is also a 1969 graduate of Gary Roosevelt High School. They are the parents of six children and five grandchildren.

MARY HILL

Indiana High School State Singles' Tennis Champion 2009

Mary Hill is an ace on the tennis court – in 2009 she won the Indiana High School Athletic Association state girls' singles title. And her high school government teacher scored an ace with her in her senior year.

Mr. Gordon, my American government teacher in twelfth grade at Munster High School, definitely surprised me. Usually, my younger teachers seemed more inexperienced and lenient. Mr. Gordon pushes all his students intellectually. Being in his classroom proved to me that I can do anything.

A 2009 graduate of Munster High School, Mary Hill is the top girls' singles player in Indiana High School Athletic Association history with a career record of 104-1. Besides winning the state girls' singles title, she also received the Mental Attitude Award in 2009. In 2006, 2007 and 2008 she helped the Munster High School girls' tennis team finish state runner-up.

LARRY HURT

1999 Indiana State Teacher of the Year

It takes a teacher to make a teacher. Larry Hurt learned that lesson from his high school arts teacher -- and went on to become the 1999 Indiana State Teacher of the Year.

I became a teacher because of the inspiration and encouragement of Mrs. Virginia Burton, who taught tenth-through twelfth-grade art at North Olmsted High School in North Olmsted, Ohio.

One day, after watching a television show about a new technique in contemporary art, I enthusiastically shared what I had seen with Mrs. Burton. She said that she thought I should tell the rest of the class about the technique. I was mortified! I was basically pretty shy and uninterested in speaking to any group. She insisted, and pulled the class together after the bell rang, telling everyone that I was going to describe a new art technique. Though unbelievably nervous, I described the process. I felt empowered. I could teach people! I decided that year that I was going to become an arts educator.

I often think of Virginia Burton as I teach art. She inspired, coaxed, cajoled, and cared. She convinced me and many other students that we had to reach for goals that we never thought possible. She also gave me permission to try and permission to fail. When I wanted to build a sculpture of glass tubing, she said try. Though the final result was pretty unsuccessful, I learned that, as an educator, I needed to encourage students to explore and attempt things even when I know the chances of success might be slim. For Virginia Burton, the journey was more important than the destination. She never said those words; she modeled them every day of her professional life. I paid attention, and it has made all the difference in my teaching career.

Larry Hurt is a perfect example of the concept "pay it forward." He says his most treasured career accomplishment is that two of his "remarkable" former students now teach art in the art department that he chairs at Ben Davis High School.

ROBIN JOST

Owner, Tilles Interiors

Who knew that eating roasted grasshoppers and crunchy ants could be a teachable moment? They're the lasting lessons Robin Jost took home from her seventh- and eighth-grade science classes at Hometown School in Hometown, Illinois – and they've fueled the curiosity that sparked her successful business career.

Chuck McCann was my middle school science teacher, a tall man with a hooked nose and a booming voice. He taught me that discovery and searching for answers was a lot more important (and more fun) than memorizing facts. He insisted on an orderly classroom, being addressed as "Sir" and keeping everything in its rightful place.

In the eighth grade we dissected sheep heads (phew!) and examined the structure of the eyeball and the brain. We went rock climbing for trilobite fossils -- and I still have a necklace made from one of the fossils! We also tried to "forge checks" on each other's checking accounts and sampled the delicacies of roasted grasshopper and crunchy ants! Every day was a new adventure and learning was so much fun.

After my experiences in Mr. McCann's class, I was always trying to figure out "How does that work and why?" That curiosity became an invaluable tool when I worked as a CPA and auditor visiting many different companies, all with varying systems and methods. Throughout my professional life I have tried to understand the business processes used and to determine what improvements could be made to make things more efficient or more accurate. This also applies to running my own business today. I think of Mr. McCann often and fondly.

Robin Jost graduated from Valparaiso University in 1977 with a B.S. in business administration and accounting. She joined Coopers & Lybrand Public Accountants after graduating, then moved to Allstate Insurance Company in 1980, and was with AAA Michigan from 1986 to 1997 as Division Manager Systems Audit. During those years she evaluated businesses for possible errors or security weaknesses to improve performance and risk avoidance.

She is now president of Tilles Interiors, a family-owned retail furniture business in Munster. "We help people beautify their homes by providing talented credentialed designers and all the top-quality furniture brands in a cozy home-like environment," she says.

Jost is a CPA, CISA (Certified Information Systems Auditor), and FLMI (Fellow of the Life Insurance Management Institute). She says her most treasured career accomplishment is "receiving my CPA certificate after three grueling days of exams at McCormick Place – I still can't drive by there (over 30 years later) without getting the chills!"

DANIEL KADLEC

Author and journalist

When his eleventh grade chemistry teacher challenged him, Daniel Kadlec got mad. But later – years later – he got smart, and realized the challenge was actually a tool to motivate him. And it worked.

I was blessed with many good and learned teachers during my school years. But there were only a few great ones; teachers who understood me and challenged and motivated me to be the best I could be. The sad thing is that only now, in my sixth decade of life, do I appreciate how much those teachers meant to me. Yet I'm guessing they'd be okay with that. For them, it was never about accolades or gratitude. They were most concerned with getting through to me and that, I think, is partly what made them great.

One teacher in particular touched me in a lifelong way. Brother Victor Winkler, a Marianist educator who taught chemistry my junior year in high school, was a crusty old guy. He had a slight hunch, wispy eyebrows, gravelly voice and a big crooked nose that supported his thick black-rimmed glasses. He spoke slowly but with a passion that illustrated and transferred his love of the subject. He over-enunciated even simple words in an almost comical fashion and he had an arsenal of quips and rhymes that usually held me rapt. If I took too long to answer a question Brother Winkler would accuse me of being "slowwwer than aaay buggg on aaay ruggg." For some reason, that always got me.

But his most potent weapon was a motivational tool that I neither saw before nor since. On the last day of class he would sit on his desk top and, chair by chair, publicly predict the grade each student would earn on their final exam. When it was my turn he looked me dead on and said, "Kadlec...hmmph...C+."

This annoyed me to no end. I was a B+ student across the board and at that moment had a B in his class. It didn't make sense. Either this was going to be the mother of all final exams or he was underestimating me. I vowed to show him up and studied like a mad man.

When my report card arrived my eyes went instantly to the chemistry mark. I had earned a B+ for the semester, which could only mean that I had aced the final and proved Old Winkler wrong. Only now, upon reflection, do I comprehend that what I really did was prove Old Winkler right. He figured I would respond to the perceived slight with redoubled determination—as surely as he figured that others with undeserved high expectations would respond with a big effort so as not to let him down. He took the time to understand which students needed a carrot and which students needed a stick. It didn't always work out. But when it did it was masterful. Brother Winkler taught me more than the periodic tables; he taught me to search for what makes people tick.

Daniel Kadlec graduated from Vianney High School in St. Louis, Missouri, and then earned a B.A. in Communications from Marquette University in Milwaukee, Wisconsin. After college, he lived in Bloomington, Indiana, for three years and was a reporter for the Bloomington Herald-Telephone newspaper.

Kadlec joined USA Today in 1986 as a business writer, and in 1992 he launched the daily column Street Talk, which anchored the newspaper's business coverage. He joined TIME magazine as a Senior Writer and columnist in 1996 and left his full-time position in 2007, when he became a contributing writer for both TIME and MONEY magazine.

He has written three books, including his most recent "With Purpose: Going from Success to Significance in Work and Life," co-authored with Ken Dychtwald and published by

HarperCollins in March 2009. He is the author of MONEY magazine's Boom Years financial column for baby boomers.

Kadlec has appeared on "The Oprah Winfrey Show," CNN, CNBC, "Good Morning America," "The Nightly Business Report" and "Wall Street Week." He won a New York Press Club award in 2002 and a National Headliner Award in 1998 for his columns on the economy and investing.

Marquette University's College of Communications recognized Kadlec with its top alumni honor, the By-Line Award, in 2005. He says one of his most treasured career accomplishments is publishing his first book, "Masters of the Universe: Winning Strategies of America's Greatest Deal Makers," in 1999. Kadlec and his wife, an executive at Johnson & Johnson, live in Chappaqua, New York, with their three children. For more, see his website at www.dankadlec.com.

GREG KAPP

Executive assistant to the president of Purdue University,
West Lafayette

The pop tune "Come On, Get Happy!" put the band The Partridge Family on the map in the '60s – and its message translated into a life lesson that Greg Kapp learned from a high school English teacher.

Ed Robertson, the freshman English teacher at Munster High School, was the most positive, encouraging and happiest person on a daily basis that I have ever met. He taught me that a positive outlook makes a huge difference!

As executive assistant to the president of Purdue University in West Lafayette, Greg Kapp says his career highlight has been playing a leadership role in successful campaigns for Purdue from 2001 to 2007.

THEODORE G. (TED) KARRAS SR.

Member, 1963 Chicago Bears World Championship Team

There was no Super Bowl when Ted Karras won the World Football Championship with the Chicago Bears in 1963, but to him the win is still as sweet today as it was back then. (Each player's take from that title game? $5,900!) And the man who put him on track to be a part of that Chicago Bears team – his high school physical education teacher and football coach in Gary – is the person who changed his life.

When I was 14 years old in 1948, my dad died. Coach Art Rolfe – the physical education teacher and football coach at Emerson High School in Gary – became a mentor to me. He advised me on many things – one being to get a good education. Since I liked football, he stressed that making good grades could help me get a scholarship to college. I was lucky enough, and following his advice, got a football scholarship to Indiana University in Bloomington.

From there I served two years in the Marines and played football for the San Diego Marines. That led to a nine-year career in the National Football League. I played with the Chicago Bears for five years and was a member of their 1963 World Championship team. After my NFL career, I taught school (physical education) and got a master's degree from Chicago State University.

I was lucky and blessed to have a wonderful person like Art Rolfe in my young life. His advice about getting as much education as you possibly can was as good then as it is today.

Ted Karras Sr. started at left guard on the Chicago Bears 1963 NFL championship team, coached by the legendary George

Halas. That Monsters of the Midway team also included Ed O'Bradovich, Doug Atkins, Bill George, Richie Pettibon, Mike Pyle, and Mike Ditka. Karras' NFL career also included stints with the Pittsburgh Steelers, Detroit Lions and Los Angeles Rams. He was inducted into the Indiana Football Hall of Fame in 1998.

CLYDE KERSEY

Indiana State Representative, District 43

His third-grade teacher turned reading into a contest – and opened a whole new world for Clyde Kersey. Now a retired teacher and state legislator, he says: "My experience as a classroom teacher has given me a better understanding of what needs to be done to improve the quality of public education in Indiana. My experience as a legislator has convinced me that we need to do everything in our power to make the lives of working men and women across this state a little easier."

The teacher who made a difference in my life was my third grade teacher, Miss Eileen Hankins. We called her Miss Eileen. She never married and devoted her life to teaching. I had a very rough start in school. I was sick much of my first year and never really caught up in the second grade. I arrived in Miss Eileen's third-grade class well behind most of my classmates. Miss Eileen announced in class one day that as soon as a student reached a certain level in reading they could take home and read a very special book that she had just purchased. I made up my mind that I was going to improve my reading until I could take Miss Eileen's book home. The test was being able to read a paragraph all the way through without any mistakes. I worked on my reading. I read to my Mom and my sisters until they were tired of listening to me. Finally, I reached the point where I was ready to take the test. I don't know who was the most surprised, me or Miss Eileen, when I passed the test. The book Miss Eileen gave me to take home and read was a book on Alexander Graham Bell, the man who invented the telephone.

I took the book home that night and I didn't even think about reading it. I had only been thinking about winning the contest. After dinner, I sat down and read the first page. I had only planned on reading a few pages and then take the book back to Miss Eileen, but after the first page, I could not put it down. I read until my Mom made me go to bed. The next morning I read a few pages while I ate breakfast and I finished the last page while waiting on the school bus.

I took the book back to Miss Eileen and asked her if she had any more books like Alexander Graham Bell. She looked at me in a strange way and said, "Are you telling me you read the entire book last night?" I said, yes, I had read the book. She then proceeded to question me about the book and I answered every question. I read all of Miss Eileen's books and she made arrangements for me to check books out of the high school library. By the time I graduated from high school, I had read most of the novels in the library.

Miss Eileen knew what she was doing in making reading into a contest. I developed a love of reading in Miss Eileen's class. She opened up a whole new world for me. I went on to graduate from Indiana State University with a Bachelor and Master of Science degrees in Social Science Education. I became a teacher and taught students the way that Miss Eileen taught me. I am now serving as a State Representative in the Indiana State Legislature. Whatever success I have had in life, I owe to Miss Eileen Hankins.

First elected to the Indiana House of Representatives in 1996, State Representative Clyde Kersey is a retired schoolteacher. He represents the citizens of Indiana House District 43 in Indianapolis.

State Rep. Kersey served in the the U.S. Air Force. He is also a member of the Indiana State Retired Teachers Association, Leadership Terre Haute, and the Harry Truman Club.

JEFFREY J. KRAJEWSKI

Co-founder, Repairtime.com

His buddies were jealous because he had a "genius" in the house to help with his homework. But to Jeff Krajewski, that "genius" was just "Dad" – the man who taught him how to think, analyze, interpret and find the resources to answer any question.

I have had the distinct privilege of having been surrounded by educators my entire life, both in the traditional sense, as well as the non-traditional. You see, my father and his two brothers were educators and education administrators. In many respects, you may say that I was enveloped in education 24/7 during my formative years.

When I reflect on all the teachers who have touched my life, influenced my direction and assisted me over the years, and there have been many, the one who stands out clearly is, ironically, the one with whom I never sat in a classroom setting – my father, Dr. Raymond J. Krajewski. He earned a Ph.D. at Purdue University and served as the vice president of academic affairs at the Calumet College of St. Joseph for many years.

I would safely say that most students, people, see education for its instrumental value, a means to an end. The how's, why's, do's and don'ts of becoming a doctor, lawyer, accountant, engineer and so forth. Education's instrumental value has been the prevalent motivator from the moment we begin school to the day we graduate. In my opinion, instrumental value is synergistic and rooted in the tangible material by-products of our education – the money, homes, cars, and toys that we collect along the way – none of which hold meaning or value when we depart this world.

My father recognized education for its intrinsic value. Intrinsic value is something that is valuable and good in and of itself. I remember growing up utterly intrigued by his wisdom and insight – a liberal arts educator at his core. I further remember my friends' envy, believing that for me homework was a "cakewalk" because I had such convenient access to this live-in genius. To the contrary, when I asked my father a question, it was met with a thought-provoking challenge, oftentimes followed up with ancillary discussion. I recall saying, "Dad, just give me the answer. I know that you know it." He never would. Rather through inquiry and challenge, he would help lead me to where the answer might be found. It was not until much later that I realized the lesson being taught. He was teaching me how to think, to analyze, to consider, interpret, and how to recognize resources holding the key to any question regardless of its origin. This discipline has proven to be an invaluable asset throughout not only my professional career, but also my life.

My father was a strong proponent of a liberal arts foundation because it provides substance for students who embrace it. Most always, it stimulates and cultivates a cognitive skill set. It provides students an opportunity to open their minds and to think beyond the tangible absolutes and to consider the heart, mind and soul, and the universe of possibilities. In the process, along the way, character may be influenced, shaped and formed. We needn't be reminded our character is the essence of who we are and, in part, at the very foundation upon which we will be judged.

My father opened the mind's eye of many students, leaving behind a legacy of thinkers and contributors to society in all corners of the world.

Jeff Krajewski is the co-founder of www.RepairTime.com, a free home repair and home improvement online referral network for homeowners. Prior to co-founding the company in 2008, he was a principal and Vice-Chairman with a commercial real estate investment firm in Scottsdale, Arizona, with an investment portfolio of nearly $500 million. He was also co-founder and Vice Chairman of a sister company that provided property management, building maintenance services, and tenant improvement build-outs for commercial real estate assets.

From 1982 to 1999, Krajewski was the principal owner of a private accounting and tax practice in Scottsdale that serviced more than 600 clients. Prior to 1982 he was a plant controller for Rand McNally & Company. He is a graduate of the Calumet College of St. Joseph and is a CPA. He says his most treasured accomplishment is earning the respect of his peers and clients.

KARIN LEE

Web site developer and designer

Every college student is looking for that "easy A" – a class you can breeze through without a second thought. Karin Lee thought she'd found just that when she signed up for a World Geography class at Valparaiso University. But to Karin's surprise, that "easy A" turned out to be something entirely different – a class led by a teacher whose story-telling skills sparked a lifelong love of travel.

While searching for an elective for a particularly busy semester at Valparaiso University, I heard that World Geography, taught by Dr. Ferencz Kallay, was an "easy A." But after enrolling in the class, I found out that it was "easy" because Professor Kallay was absolutely captivating. He had a wonderful way of telling stories. His lectures were fascinating accounts of the countries and regions of the world, and the people he met through his travels. He inspired in me an interest and a lifelong curiosity in different cultures and far-away places. In the end, that's proven to be far more valuable than the grade that I earned in Dr. Kallay's class.

I've had the opportunity to visit parts of Asia, the Middle East, and Europe for work, as well as for pleasure. Each trip reminds me of that World Geography class. And that prompts me to dream about the next place in our great big world that I want to explore. Thank you, Dr. Kallay!

A 1977 graduate of Valparaiso University, Karin Lee says her most treasured career accomplishment is managing the design and development of a multi-language website for The Ritz-Carlton Hotel Company.

NORMAN L. LOWERY

President and CEO, First Financial Bank,
and CEO, First Financial Corporation

A high school football coach who instilled the value of teamwork – not only on the playing field, but in life as well – remains an inspiration to Norman Lowery.

Many athletes have fond memories of their coaches. Such is the case with Claude "Woody" Roloff and the hundreds of athletes who crossed his path in the early '60s when he was the football coach at Gerstmeyer High School in Terre Haute. These young men from low- to moderate-income families with working parents were provided with "coaching" beyond the times. But more importantly they were also taught the importance of honesty, integrity, respect for their opponent and hard work.

Winning was important, but not winning at any cost. Woody taught us the importance of a team, to trust one another and to pick each other up when one of us was knocked down. To Woody, these principles were key to a successful team, but more importantly were essential for life. The world needs more Woody Roloffs.

Norman Lowery is currently President and Chief Executive Officer of First Financial Bank, and CEO of First Financial Corporation in Terre Haute. A former practicing attorney with Wright, Shagley & Lowery, he was named an Indiana State University Distinguished Alumni in 2001 and has been on the ISU Board of Trustees since 2007.

RICHARD LUGAR

United States Senator

During more than four decades as a public servant, Richard Lugar has been interviewed by journalists countless times, and been quoted in newspapers and magazines around the world. But he learned his first lesson about freedom of the press when a column that he wrote for his high school newspaper touched a nerve with the School Board – and the paper's faculty advisor stepped in to smooth things over.

One of the most memorable teachers in my life was Jean Grubb. She was the faculty advisor of Shortridge High School's Daily Echo when I was a Thursday columnist for the paper. I'm fortunate to have been among the hundreds of students in her 46 years of teaching that benefited from her kindness, wise counsel, and steadfast concern for the well-being of others.

As a high school student, the opportunity to publish a column, and to know that at least a few of my classmates read what I had written, provided an unparalleled privilege. On one occasion, an unflattering column that I authored about the unhealthy habits of the basketball team was read by the Indianapolis School Board - who only received copies of the paper's Thursday edition. This incident caused a temporary shutdown of the Echo's headquarters and a sudden trip to the principal's office. They wanted me to understand the consequences that unbridled journalism could have on myself, the school, and Jean.

Throughout this life experience, Jean was my heroine. And ultimately, freedom of the press prevailed. In my Senate office, I still keep a bound volume of Daily Echo's from my four years as a columnist nearby.

In 2005, Jean deservedly received the Lifetime Achievement Award from the Indiana High School Press

Association for her tireless commitment to journalistic excellence among young people, and her unwavering support of the alumni and history of Shortridge High School.

I am honored to recognize Jean for the important influence which she had on my life, and thank her for her exemplary dedication to teaching.

Richard Lugar graduated first in his class at both Shortridge High School in Indianapolis in 1950 and Denison University in Granville, Ohio, in 1954. He attended Pembroke College at Oxford University as a Rhodes Scholar, receiving a graduate degree in 1956. He served in the U.S. Navy from 1957 to 1960. Sen. Lugar is also an Eagle Scout and is a recipient of the Distinguished Eagle Scout Award from the Boy Scouts of America.

After serving on the Indianapolis Board of School Commissioners from 1964 to 1967, he was elected mayor of Indianapolis in 1967 at age 35, and was reelected in 1971. He was elected to the United States Senate as a Republican in 1976. He served as Chairman of the Senate Committee on Foreign Relations from 1985 to 1987 and 2003 to 2007. Much of his work in the Senate has been aimed at dismantling nuclear, biological and chemical weapons around the world.

In 2006, TIME magazine selected Lugar as one of America's 10 Best Senators. He is now the most senior Republican in the Senate.

Sen. Lugar manages his family's 604-acre corn, soybean and tree farm in Marion County.

LLOYD McCLENDON

Little League World Series record holder

Lloyd McClendon holds the one record in baseball that might never be broken – he homered in five consecutive at-bats in the 1971 Little League World Series, earning the nickname "Legendary Lloyd." He met his favorite teacher at Gary Roosevelt High School.

Benny Dorsey taught me to stand tall, be proud of who I am and where I came from and to always believe in me!

Lloyd McClendon was drafted by the New York Mets out of Valparaiso University and broke into the major leagues as an outfielder with the Cincinnati Reds in 1987. He also played for the Chicago Cubs and Pittsburgh Pirates. After retiring from playing, he served as a hitting coach for the Pirates until he was appointed manager after the 2000 season, a position he held until September 2005. Since 2007, he has been the hitting coach for the Detroit Tigers.

EDWIN W. MILLER

Chairman and CEO, Millennium Capital Group

A teacher who was small in stature ended up leaving a giant impression on Edwin Miller.

Although Professor Susan Cummings was just a wisp of a person, who carried a bag of books and materials that was almost as big as her, she made a huge impression on her sophomore English students at Indiana State University. She transformed a standard course in English into an introduction to great works of literature, art, and music. More importantly she challenged each of us to think about what each work meant and why it was of significance. She planted the seed in each student that learning would be a lifelong experience and responsibility. Each time she opened a new door to us, she challenged us to consider its implications. What an inspiration she was! She touched the lives of so many and we carry her lessons within each of us.

Edwin Miller is now chairman and CEO of Millennium Capital Group.

SPIRO B. MITSOS

Retired co-founder, National Health Care Corp.

A college professor put Spiro Mitsos on the path to pursue a graduate degree – starting a professional and personal bond that endured for nearly 50 years.

Dr. Rutherford Porter, a practicing school psychologist, came to Indiana State University as head of the Department of Special Education. I started my undergraduate studies in special education in the late 1940s. Thus began a friendship-mentor-colleague relationship that lasted almost 50 years.

During my undergraduate years, Bert was a teacher, advisor, counselor, role model and friend. He encouraged me to pursue graduate studies which culminated with me earning my Ph.D. in psychology from Purdue University in 1955.

I remained in Indiana for my entire career in clinical practice spanning 50 years. This afforded many opportunities for collegial interaction with Bert. We served together on the Board of Directors of the Indiana Psychological Association. During my term as president, he was my elder statesman.

Now retired, I still look back with gratitude to Dr. Rutherford Porter.

Spiro Mitsos is co-founder of National Health Care Corp Res-Care Inc.

ARDEN MOORE

Author, radio talk show host and magazine editor

It was hate at first sight when Arden Moore walked into Janice Dean's eighth-grade English class. But eventually those feelings thawed – and when Moore ran away from home to escape her abusive stepmother, she headed to Mrs. Dean's house. Today Moore credits Mrs. Dean's special talents for building the foundations of her successful journalism career.

So much for the validity of clichés. My first impression of my favorite teacher was far from magical – but I blame myself. The first time I met Janice Dean was second semester of eighth grade at Taft Junior High School in Crown Point. Our ultra cool advanced English teacher who let us eat pizza on Fridays and would darken the room while playing records of Edgar Allan Poe novels mysteriously did not return to our class following the Christmas holiday break.

In his place was Mrs. Dean wearing an anything but trendy dress and sporting big-framed glasses and a no-nonsense demeanor. Goodbye, Friday pizzas. Hello, monthly book reports! I tried to despise her in my awkward, quiet eighth-grader way but deep down inside, I knew I was learning how to conjugate verbs, put the brakes on run-on sentences and identify protagonists in literary classics.

When the bell sounded for summer recess, I thought, "Good riddance, Mrs. Dean!" – and enjoyed the summer before starting my freshman year at Crown Point High School. I discovered I really loved writing and signed up to be on the Inklings, the school's bi-weekly newspaper. I strode into the newspaper office to meet the advisor and found – you guessed it! – Mrs. Dean. She had transferred to the high school over the summer break to teach English and serve as the newspaper advisor.

Working on the school newspaper, I got the chance to see another side of Mrs. Dean. She knew how to spot a news story, how to recruit a staff and most importantly, how to bring out the best in each of us. Thanks to her, I learned to answer the "why" in every story I submitted and to always verify facts. I learned not to pre-judge people by their outward appearances and to never "pre-write" a story until I finished reporting.

During my high school years, my home life was unsettling. My dad traveled a lot and my stepmom physically abused my brother and me. One time during my senior year, I took my bruised body and "ran away" to Mrs. Dean's house. She and her husband helped me to maintain my focus on my future as a journalist and to never give up.

The day I graduated from high school, I left my negative home situation to temporarily live with my older sister. Mrs. Dean was always just a phone call away to give me pep talks as I somehow managed to work full-time at a local newspaper and attend college full-time and graduate in four years.

Since college, I've spent 20 years as a newspaper reporter and editor for major dailies and another 10 as a magazine editor, author and radio show host. For each new success or mastery in journalism, I credit Mrs. Dean for seeing my potential and for reminding me to do my best – despite life's challenges. My first impression of Mrs. Dean was lousy, but my lasting impression of her special talents will always be treasured.

Arden Moore wears many collars in the pet world: best-selling author, magazine editor, radio show host, professional speaker and animal behavior consultant. She's known as "America's Pet Edu-Tainer"™, and is an in-demand guest on countless radio and TV shows, including "CNN Headline News," "Fox News" and Martha Stewart Living Radio.

Moore serves as editor of "Catnip," a national monthly publication, and editor-at-large of "Fido Friendly" magazine.

She hosts a popular weekly radio show called "Oh Behave!" on www.PetLifeRadio.com.

Moore has authored 19 books on dogs and cats. To learn more, visit www.ArdenMoore.com.

MARK MORGAN

Vice President, Business Planning and Administration, Bayer Health Care

As Mark Morgan has learned, even a kindergarten teacher can have a lasting impact on a child who needs to know he is important.

May Jean Rose, my kindergarten Sunday school teacher at the First Baptist Church in Vincennes, Indiana, took five minutes to tell me that my life was important. My family was dysfunctional. This encouragement enabled me to overcome many obstacles and have confidence to build a successful life.

Mark Morgan graduated from Indiana State University with a B.S. in accounting and has been honored by the school as a Distinguished Alumni. He also holds an MBA from Illinois State University. He's currently vice president of business planning and administration for Bayer Health Care, and has over 30 years' professional experience in finance leadership roles with top tier firms including Pfizer, SC Johnson Wax and Mylan Pharmaceuticals.

Morgan is an avid gardener, outdoorsman and writer. He is also a cancer survivor, and says he's most proud of being a successful father and husband while building a career.

JAMES G. "Jay" MOSELEY

President, Franklin College

A young baseball fan grew up to be a college president –
thanks to an open-minded math teacher who made learning fun.

My sixth-grade math teacher excused me from class for
the entire year and let me keep up-to-date baseball statistics –
thereby helping me learn lots of math and teaching me that
learning can be truly enjoyable.

A college ethics teacher, Robert MacAfee Brown, taught
me that learning becomes significant when it improves the lives
of other people.

And a graduate school theology professor, Schubert M.
Ogden, taught me how a student should prepare as well for class
as the teacher does – thereby helping me prepare to be a teacher
when it was my turn.

President Moseley is Franklin College's 15th president.
Prior to joining the college in 2002, he was vice president and
dean of the college and a professor of religion at Transylvania
University. He holds a bachelor's degree from Stanford
University and a doctorate and master's degree from the
University of Chicago Divinity School. He is the author of three
books and numerous scholarly articles about religion in
American life and culture.

He says his most treasured accomplishment is seeing
former students who are serving others in significant ways.

JOHN P. NEWTON

Vice President, Indiana State University Foundation

A first-year teacher reached out to the "new kid" in his sixth-grade class, and created a lifelong leader.

The fall of 1958 was George Thompson's first year of teaching at Thornton Elementary School in Terre Haute. He was in his late 20s, had been in the U.S. Army for two years, and had worked part-time at Commercial Solvents and went to Indiana State Teachers College full-time to earn his degree in elementary education. The Vigo County schools consolidated the same year and I was "transferred" from Sugar Grove to Thornton. I was the "new kid" in my sixth-grade class; other students were barely friendly. On the second day of class Mr. Thompson announced the officers of the School Patrol (the most prestigious position in the school!). He named the Sergeants, the Lieutenants and then me as Captain. All the other kids "hated" me for the next three weeks!

Outside of my family, Mr. Thompson was the first person to see in me leadership potential . . . I'll always be grateful.

John P. Newton has served Indiana State University for 35 years. Now vice president of the ISU Foundation, he's been associate director, director and executive director of the ISU Alumni Association, and vice president for Alumni and Constituent Relations for the Foundation.

SANDRA R. PATTERSON-RANDLES

Chancellor, Indiana University Southeast in New Albany

He called her a "fresh breeze blowing in from the Colorado mountains" – and Dr. Sandra Patterson-Randles felt an immediate connection to Dr. Louis J. Swift. Her favorite teacher is now emeritus professor of classics and associate provost for undergraduate studies at the University of Kentucky, Lexington.

I have known Lou Swift nearly all of my professional life. I first met him 37 years ago when I was just beginning graduate school at the University of Kentucky. After our initial conversation about my background and travels, he commented that I was a "fresh breeze blowing in from the Colorado mountains," and I felt an immediate connection to this very kind, positive, and supportive man. He helped me get a much-needed job in academia and then taught me in classics courses and mentored me through two master's degrees and a doctorate. He has served as my teacher, teaching colleague, departmental supervisor and all-around advisor for stages in my career ranging from graduate teaching assistant to university chancellor. He is the quintessential teacher/scholar whose academic leadership and high standards have molded hundreds of students into top-notch professionals. Moreover, Lou is one of the finest human beings I have ever known. He will always be my role model.

Dr. Sandra Patterson-Randles began her duties as Chancellor of Indiana University Southeast on July 1, 2002. She earned a bachelor's degree in classical languages and literature from the University of Colorado at Boulder and two master's degrees in English and in classical languages and literatures, as well as a doctorate in English, from the University of Kentucky.

Dr. Patterson-Randles has taught from the high school to graduate level in higher education and has held teaching or administrative positions in six states at eight different institutions.

Before coming to IU Southeast, Chancellor Patterson-Randles served for four years as vice president for academic affairs at the University of Pittsburgh at Johnstown, and spent 10 years at Western State College in Gunnison, Colorado, where she was chair of the Department of Modern Languages.

She says her most treasured accomplishment is successfully teaching the full range of St. John's College Great Books courses.

MIKE PETTIBONE

Superintendent, Adams Central Community Schools

Coming from a broken home, Mike Pettibone appreciated the welcoming hand of an elementary school teacher – who went on to become his boss and mentor.

When I was 12, my parents divorced and my mother moved from Decatur, Indiana, to the neighboring town of Bluffton. Mr. Ken Payne was not even one of my classroom teachers; rather he was a welcoming adult into a strange new school. His smiles and words of encouragement gave me enough encouragement to keep returning. Mr. Payne then left to take an administrative role in a neighboring district. Yet he kept that quiet positive encouragement. Mr. Payne ended up as a superintendent … and gave me my first teaching position, my first principal-ship, and then as a retired superintendent, mentored me for my first several years – WOW!

Mike Pettibone has served as an elementary teacher, high school coach, elementary school principal, high school principal, and school superintendent. He says his most treasured accomplishment has been being recognized by the Indiana Council for Exceptional Children as the state's Outstanding Building Administrator.

PHILIP POTEMPA

Columnist, The Times of Northwest Indiana

Like Clark Kent, Phil Potempa grew up on a farm and went on to work at a large metropolitan newspaper. And while he doesn't have that mild-mannered reporter's Superman alter ego, Potempa credits his mother's encouragement and a high school business teacher for pushing him to look beyond the boundaries of the small farm town where he grew up.

My mother always encouraged me to be a leader and be assertive.

Those skills developed much further by the time I reached high school and met Janet Hetterscheidt, one of the business department teachers at the North Judson-San Pierre Schools. She also served as the faculty adviser for the Student Council, the elected student government organization.

She encouraged me to run for one of the Student Council positions, and even after I lost after a tough election, she encouraged me not to give up. Not only did I eventually get my chance at a Student Council member seat, but by the time I was a junior in high school, I was the Student Council vice president. And by the time I was in my senior year, I was elected student body president.

Mrs. Hetterscheidt was a teacher who made even the toughest and most tedious of responsibilities fun. She also taught me an important lesson that I still value today: "It's not always what you know in this world. It's also who you know."

I will always be grateful to Mrs. Hetterscheidt for providing advice and direction, which pushed me to rise above average standards, and also reminding me to push myself to raise my own standards to strive for every goal, no matter how lofty it might seem.

Mrs. Hetterscheidt, who was still teaching as of 2009 after three decades, was one of the first teachers to introduce me to the opportunities that awaited me. She also highlighted a world that existed far beyond the small farming town that gave me such a great start in life.

Phil Potempa grew up in San Pierre, graduated from Valparaiso University in 1992 and is a columnist for The Times of Northwest Indiana.

He shares memories of his rural youth and family stories in his weekly column "From the Farm." Those columns have inspired two semi-autobiographical books, "From the Farm: Family Recipes and Memories of a Lifetime," and "More From the Farm: Family Recipes and Memories of a Lifetime."

WILLIAM PULLINSI

Artistic Director, Theatre at the Center

Dinner and a movie has always been a popular date night, but the concept of dinner and a play – together! -- was dreamed up by William Pullinsi who credits a college theater professor for guiding his career.

Harlan Grant taught a college theater course at Boston Conservatory, and was a great historian of theater, especially early New England theater. Harlan was a principal actor and director as well as a great teacher. He brought great humanity and insight to his work, and passed on many special traditions to his students.

William Pullinsi is the founder and artistic director of Candelight Playhouse, America's first dinner theater, which opened in Washington, D.C., in 1959 and Summit, Illinois, in 1961. He has served as Artistic Director at Theatre at the Center in Munster since 2005. He has directed and/or produced more than 400 shows in his career, receiving 18 Jeff Awards from the Chicago theatre community.

Pullinsi received his B.F.A. from Boston Conservatory, did graduate work at the Goodman School and received the honorary degree of Doctor of Humanities from Lewis University. He was named a Distinguished Artist in the Theatre by the Chicago Academy of Arts and also by the Chicago Drama League.

Pullinsi says his most treasured accomplishment is introducing many productions to Chicago audiences that would otherwise never have been seen in the area while he was the producer/director of Candlelight Playhouse.

PATRICK RALSTON

Former Director, Indiana Department of Natural Resources

When a fourth-grade teacher helped Patrick Ralston be above-average, she nurtured a future public servant.

Mrs. Trench, my fourth-grade teacher at Warren School in Terre Haute, was the type of teacher who made you want to learn. She was a very special person to me. She made me want to attend school. She took an interest in trying to help me be above average.

Patrick Ralston graduated from Indiana State University with a bachelor's degree in 1972 and a master's degree in 1973. He was awarded ISU's Distinguished Alumni Award in 1996. He was the Director of Parks and Recreation in Butler from 1973 to 1974, Regional Supervisor of Indiana State Parks from 1974 to 1979, and Supervisor of Parks, Recreation and Cemeteries in Terre Haute from 1978 to 1989. He became Director of the Indiana Department of Natural Resources in 1989. He has also served as chairman of the Great Lakes Commission, Executive Director of Indiana's Emergency Management and Fire and Building, and Public Safety Training Foundation, and Executive Director of the National Resources Foundation.

DR. GERALD M. "JERRY" REAVEN, M.D.

Professor Emeritus, Stanford University

Nearly everyone has heard of "The Joy of Cooking" – the famous cookbook that's sold over 18 million copies. But the joy of learning? That's the lesson Jerry Reaven took home from his teachers in elementary, junior high and high school – and it sparked an award-winning career in medicine.

I've thought long and hard, and I still don't feel able to identify my "favorite" teacher. I can remember many teachers at each stage of my life that were important to me, and several of them contributed at each of these junctures to the path I eventually followed.

I attended Washington Elementary School, Junior High and High School in the Indiana Harbor neighborhood of East Chicago from 1937 to 1944. During this time several teachers introduced me to the joy associated with the process of learning. They made it clear to me that pursuing academic goals was not only acceptable, but something to eagerly seek out.

I left Indiana Harbor and the Washington school system in 1944, and spent the next five years as an undergraduate at the University of Chicago. Essentially, every teacher I had there was extraordinary, but they all had one thing in common. They did their best to insist that I think for myself, that I had the right, in fact, the responsibility to challenge accepted ideas. No matter how hallowed the authority figure, I had the obligation to evaluate their views, not accepting on faith that they must be right. This point of view was essential to me as a clinical scientist; if I could challenge Aristotle, I certainly did not have to accept as dogma what was printed in the "New England Journal of Medicine."

In 1949 I entered Medical School at the University of Chicago. It was there that I first met physicians who were clinically astute, but also capable of being both great teachers and research scientists. For the first time in my life I recognized a potential career that I believed would keep me happy and occupied throughout the remainder of my life.

I have been able to live that dream, but there is no doubt in my mind that any success I might have had would not have been possible without the teachers in Indiana Harbor who introduced me to the zest for learning, and the faculty at the University of Chicago who made it quite clear that it was more than acceptable to challenge accepted points of view.

Dr. Jerry Reaven says his most treasured career accomplishment is "being lucky enough to have spent my entire career in a School of Medicine, where I have been able to be a clinician, teacher and investigator."

After earning his medical degree at the University of Chicago, he did research work at Stanford University in California and served two years in the U.S. Army medical corps. He completed his residency at the University of Michigan. Dr. Reaven then took up a U.S. Public Health Service research post at Stanford and became a full professor in 1970. He's now professor emeritus in medicine there.

He's best known for calling attention to "Syndrome X," a cluster of conditions that may indicate a predisposition to diabetes, hypertension and heart disease.

Dr. Reaven is a member of several research organizations and has received numerous prizes for his research achievements. He is co-author of a popular book on Syndrome X and its repercussions on cardiovascular disease.

DENNIS C. RITTENMEYER

President, Calumet College of St. Joseph

A car put Dennis Rittenmeyer on his life's path. And not just any car -- it was a 1956 Chevrolet convertible. But it wasn't really the car that put Rittenmeyer on the road to higher education. It was the car's driver -- a seventh-grade biology teacher who made a lasting impact on his life. Rittenmeyer eventually majored in biology, and even called his teacher for advice as an adult. Today Rittenmeyer still sees his favorite teacher.

The most influential teacher in my life was Mr. William Cope. Bill has retired more than once, and most recently (I believe) served as an interim principal at Hanover High School.

My first encounter with Mr. Cope was as a student enrolled in a seventh-grade biology class at Hobart Junior High School. I was a typical male seventh-grader, consumed by all of the issues that intrigue seventh-graders, but not school issues. My experience with teachers up to that point had been that they were always much older and wiser, but I never felt very close to any of them.

Mr. Cope was different, though. I believe he had only recently graduated from college, and so by age, he was much younger than any teacher I can remember. Not only that, he was driving a 1956 Chevrolet convertible with a continental kit. Since I loved cars at that time, and still do, Mr. Cope made an immediate impression upon me. He was different. He was cool!

Mr. Cope was also a coach, and so in that year and the years until I graduated from Hobart High School, I encountered him on the baseball field and the football field. He was always cool. I don't believe he gave me any special or preferential treatment, but I always felt "good" when I was around him.

After graduation, I attended Western Michigan University and quickly realized that I had to declare a major. Not having given it much thought prior to that time, when the time came to make the decision (late in my freshman year) I chose to become a biology major and a baseball coach.

I never taught biology and I never coached baseball. After graduating with those licenses, I chose to work in higher education and have remained in higher education to this day.

While I lived out of the area for many years, I would return on holidays because my parents lived in Hobart. During these times, I would hear from my father periodically about Bill Cope's activities. Indeed, they even had a common vacation spot in Michigan.

When I had the opportunity to return to Indiana in 1985, I tried to determine where I wanted to live with my two young daughters. Schools with female soccer programs became one of my residential criteria, and I called Bill Cope for advice. He was the only person I knew who still lived in Hobart, and whose advice I could count on being accurate.

I still see Bill periodically. I even asked once if he wanted to supervise some of our student teachers at Calumet College of St. Joseph. He didn't. He has heard me make presentations on economic development and educational issues over the years, and he is always very gracious. He seems to like to see me, and I like to see him. And, I still remember the 1956 Chevrolet convertible with the continental kit.

Dr. Dennis Rittenmeyer received his bachelor's and master's degrees from Western Michigan University and his Ph.D. in Higher Education Administration from Michigan State University.

He began his career as a resident director at Michigan State, and aside from a two-year stint as Captain in the U.S. Army, he has spent the last 40 years in higher education. He is the first lay president of Calumet College of St. Joseph, a position he's held since 1986. He currently serves as chairman of the Northwest Indiana Quality of Life Council and has previously served as president of the Tri-City Mental Health Board of Directors.

AMY D. SHOJAI

Author and certified animal behavior consultant

The sound of music filled Amy Shojai's childhood – and it was her take-no-prisoners high school choir teacher who gave her the skills to succeed in life.

Music has always been a part of my life. My father is a retired elementary school music teacher, and I began piano lessons in second grade, cello in fifth grade, and voice in middle school. I have performed in school, community and professional music productions for more than 35 years. But it was my choir teacher at Elkhart Central High School, Bill Gowdy, I credit with giving me the confidence and guidance to succeed as a performer.

Mr. Gowdy was a take-no-prisoners teacher who demanded excellence and got it. His students attended before- and after-school rehearsals as a matter of course. He offered individual coaching for solo and ensemble, pushed us to challenge ourselves as a group, and gave up his lunch hours to teach a non-credit class on theory that students requested. Mr. Gowdy encouraged me to pursue music with private lessons, pushed me to audition for elite performance groups, and beamed when his students (including me) succeeded.

Mr. Gowdy died during my senior year, right after the Christmas concert, and the entire music department went into mourning. He'd taught there I think 40 years or so. I only recently realized how much he gave to helping students achieve success, time and effort well above the parameters of the job.

Because of Mr. Gowdy's influence, music helped develop my confidence in public speaking and professional interactions; taught me the benefits of collaborative efforts; reinforced the notion that positive results require dedication and practice; and the discipline I learned through music has translated into positives in every aspect of my life today.

Amy D. Shojai was raised in Indiana, and attended school in Bristol, Elkhart and Goshen College. She is a certified animal behavior consultant and nationally known authority on pet care and behavior. She began her career as a veterinary technician and is the award-winning author of 22 non-fiction pet books and more than 1,000 published articles and columns. She also hosts a weekly half-hour Internet radio "podcast" called "Pet Peeves."

In addition to a weekly "PETiQuette" newspaper column, she writes a weekly column at the Purina Cat Chow web site and produces the free monthly E-newsletter Pet Peeves. She has been a newsletter columnist for Sergeant's Pet Care, and the dog and cat behavior columnist for www.HomeAgain.com. Shojai also hosts a forum at www.iVillage.com, served as the official "Cat Blogger" for the NBC Universal Television website www.Petside.com, and as a feature writer for www.PetsBest.com.

She is the founder and current president of the International Cat Writers' Association, a certified member of the International Association of Animal Behavior Consultants, Dog Writer's Association of America, Inc., a past president of Oklahoma Writers Federation, Inc., and a member of International Thriller Writers.

TAVIS SMILEY

Broadcaster, author, advocate and philanthropist

When Tavis Smiley started second grade in Bunker Hill, Indiana, he was the only black student in his classroom. He'd just moved with his family from Gulfport, Mississippi, where he was born, and he felt like an outsider. He wasn't motivated – until his teacher, a white woman named Mrs. Graft, convinced him that he was special. In this excerpt from his best-selling book, "What I Know for Sure: My Story of Growing Up in America" published by Doubleday, Smiley recalls how Mrs. Graft changed his attitude about himself.

I looked out the window from my second-grade classroom and watched the rains wash over the cornfields. The wind blew so strongly I wondered if the stalks would break as they swayed and bent.

"You seem very far away, Tavis," said Mrs. Vera Graft, my grade school teacher. "You look like you're daydreaming again."

Mama had already been to school to speak to Mrs. Graft. The only time Mom missed church, in fact, was for a teacher's conference. She'd informed me that Mrs. Graft wasn't happy with my performance or attitude. I just wasn't motivated. The only way I'd learned my multiplication was by Mom cracking my knuckles at night.

I'd had a hard time adjusting to school in Indiana. In Mississippi, my classmates were all black. My preschool teacher, Mrs. Warren, a black woman who brought out the best in her students, had encouraged me.

Here, though, all my classmates and teachers were white. As the only black student in the class, I felt like an outsider. After class, Mrs. Graft came over to my desk.

"You have a bright and alert mind," Mrs. Graft told me sternly, but like Mama, with a caring tone. "You're gifted with a fine intelligence, Tavis, but you have to apply it. When we read, you act like you're not interested. When we do arithmetic, you act like you don't care. I don't think you're trying hard enough."

I couldn't look Mrs. Graft in the eye. I knew she was right. Glancing out the window, I could see a rainbow arched over the sky from one end of the world to the other.

"When you look at that magnificent rainbow, Tavis," she said, following my gaze, "think of the beauty that lies ahead of you. Your life will be full of beauty, because you are a beautiful person. You can achieve whatever you want to achieve. You can follow that rainbow—do wonderful things, meet wonderful people, see wonderful places. There are no limits on what you can do. You're different from the others in this class, Tavis. The color of your skin is different. But listen to me when I say that you are just as smart, if not smarter, and just as good as anyone here. And I mean *anyone*. It's time to quit quitting, Tavis. Deep down, I know you're not a quitter. You're an achiever. And if you work at it, you're going to get that pot at the end of the rainbow."

As I did my homework that night, Mrs. Graft's words echoed inside me. As I attended choir rehearsal, as I helped Smiley & Sons clean up barracks on the base, her words replayed in my mind: *Time to quit quitting*.

That night I dreamed of rainbows—thousands of Technicolor rainbows illuminating fields of gold.

You can achieve your heart's desire.

You can get that pot at the end of the rainbow.

I knew Mrs. Graft was right.

Looking back, I now understand that not all kids are motivated to achieve. I wasn't. I needed encouragement. I needed someone to take special interest in me. It was significant that, for a black child in an overwhelmingly white environment, that interest came from a white teacher. Mrs. Graft was telling me that I was as good as anyone, white or black. She showed me that a single mentor, especially an early one, can transform your

114

attitude about yourself. On the deepest level, she was showing me love.

Tavis Smiley hosts the late-night television talk show "Tavis Smiley" on PBS, and "The Tavis Smiley Show" distributed by Public Radio International (PRI). In addition to his radio and television work, Smiley's memoir "What I Know For Sure: My Story of Growing Up in America" became a New York Times bestseller, and the book he edited "Covenant with Black America," became the first non-fiction book by a black-owned publisher to reach #1 on the New York Times' bestseller list.

TIME magazine honored Smiley in 2009 as one of "The World's 100 Most Influential People." In 1999 he founded the Tavis Smiley Foundation, a nonprofit organization that provides leadership training and development for the next generation of leaders. His communications company, The Smiley Group, Inc., is dedicated to supporting human rights and related empowerment issues.

Smiley's achievements have earned him numerous awards and honorary doctorate degrees, including one from his alma mater, Indiana University, and the Du Bois Medal from Harvard University's W.E.B. Du Bois Institute for African and African American Research.

To learn more about Smiley, go to his web site www.TavisSmiley.com.

QUENTIN P. SMITH

Member of the Tuskegee Airmen

Music legend Nat King Cole played at East Chicago Washington High School's segregated prom in 1935 – all because jazz lover Quentin Smith's high school band teacher assigned him to play the clarinet.

My favorite teacher during my East Chicago Washington High School years was Eugene Creitz – a band teacher. I selected band because this was the age of Duke Ellington, Cab Calloway and Jimmie Lunceford. I chose the saxophone because of Charlie Parker and the other great saxophonists. Mr. Creitz asked me if I had a sax. I said no. He said, "Then you will play what I tell you to play. You will play a clarinet." We practiced all year. We kept the horns all summer. We played as groups in our homes. Not in mine – too many people. When my turn came in the summer, Mr. Creitz let us play at his home.

When we marched at games we played without music. We made letters of our school and the opposing school on the field. When we gave concerts, the auditorium was filled. One day Mr. Creitz told me he had sent in my name to play in the 1933 World's Fair Band/Orchestra of Students In-And-About Chicago. Two weeks later he said I was selected. There was another student there who could play pretty good also. His name was Cole – Nat Cole. We became friends. When I graduated in 1935 he played for our segregated prom.

I could not go to college the year I graduated. My parents could not afford it, even though I had a few scholarships. There were no Pell Grants then. I worked, saved my money and went to Indiana State University in 1936. Again, I signed up for band.

The professor asked me what did I play. Did I play the tuba? The big brass drum? I had no horn with me. I felt ashamed when I told him I played the clarinet – and didn't own one. He gave me the opportunity to play a musical piece after sterilizing a reed and a mouthpiece. As I was playing, he was listening for tone as well as facility. He looked at me. I looked at him, continually playing without the music. He said, "You got another horn." My training under Mr. Creitz scored again.

After graduating from Indiana State University, Quentin Smith became an English teacher at Roosevelt High School in Gary. In 1942 he enlisted in the Army Air Force, and became a pilot and trainer in the Tuskegee Airmen – the famed World War 2 corps of African-American fighter pilots. Smith also took a lead step in the process that led to integration of the Armed Forces. After being denied entry to the whites-only officer's club at Freeman Air Field near Seymour, Smith and other black Air Corps officers refused to sign a decree approving the club's segregation.

Smith served as the first principal of Gary's West Side High School and later as director of secondary education for the Gary schools. For 35 years, he was also a trustee of Calumet College of St. Joseph.

JOHN P. SMYTH

Former member, U.S. Olympic Committee,
and former director, USOC Olympic Training Centers

One small-town Indiana boy who loved sports stepped into the life of another small-town Indiana boy who loved sports -- and impacted the lives of countless Olympic athletes.

From 1961 to 1965, my alma mater went from Indiana State Teachers College to Indiana State College to Indiana State University. During those same four years I grew in a most similar fashion. I went from a small-town boy without any career direction or inspiration to a college graduate with a good academic preparation, experience in the field through an undergraduate assistantship and a solid concept of a college professor and program administrator from my class instructor, academic advisor and intramural program director.

Jim Wittenauer was a relatively young instructor on the faculty at Indiana State Teachers College in 1961. Starting with our first meeting to develop my first semester curriculum, Jim helped me transition from a small school honor student and perennial class president with no clue about a course of study or career path to a college graduate with sufficient education and experience to earn my first position as a professor on a college faculty. He followed up his undergraduate support by offering me a graduate assistantship upon completion of my bachelor's degree. His advice regarding how much easier that degree would be if taken immediately following the undergraduate degree proved true and it also broadened my opportunities to secure a college position.

It was Jim's modeling of professionalism, clarity of purpose, selfless service, understanding of the teacher-student relationship, and later as a role model in the intramural program where he delegated responsibility and authority in equal measure. Jim prepared his class assignments in challenging, but manageable units which were both effective and efficient in their design and implementation. Jim's relaxed and humble demeanor brought him close to the students, yet he maintained the professional relationship between himself and his students and easily earned the respect of each. Jim was knowledgeable about the course material for each of the several classes I took under him, but his effectiveness was due in equal measure to his skill in sharing the information.

Jim and I were alike in many ways. We were both small-town Indiana boys who loved all sports, we were influenced greatly by caring parents and our religious beliefs, and we were probably similar in our academic abilities. But, we were different in some ways as well. Jim was a Chicago Cubs fan and I loved my Cardinals. He was of the Catholic faith and I was a Methodist. He was married with three children and I was single for the first two years of college.

We were drawn together by a love of sport and a belief that all students, not just varsity athletes, deserved an opportunity to compete and cooperate in a varied, structured sports program. He had a love of learning that was modeled rather than touted or flaunted. He was grounded by his faith and personal values. I wanted to be like Jim – he wanted me to be more. He took me to my first national convention and demonstrated how to give back to the profession.

To this day, we remain friends, but Jim remains humbly bewildered by my appreciation of his influence. Jim was an effective and efficient teacher, a competent and caring administrator, and a faculty advisor who walked beside me in the four years of my greatest personal growth.

Dr. John P. Smyth earned his B.S. and M.S. degrees and his P.E.D. in physical education at Indiana State University, where his favorite teacher, Dr. James L. Wittenauer, was a professor and also the school's intramural sports director. Smyth was named an ISU Distinguished Alumni in 1999.

He served the United States Olympic Committee for 10 years as director of the USOC Olympic Training Centers in Colorado Springs, Colorado; Lake Placid, New York; Chula Vista, California, and Marquette, Michigan. He was also Director of USOC High Performance Center at the Olympic Games site in 2000, 2002 and 2004.

From 1966 to 1994 Dr. Smyth held a number of positions at The Citadel, including professor, deputy director of the Citadel Summer Camp for Boys, and the department head of the Health and Physical Education Department. He is now a professor emeritus there.

GAYLE SPIESS

Software developer

Did you know that if you bite your fingernails, they'll stick to your appendix? Well, of course, they don't. But Gayle Spiess "learned" that fun lesson from her third-grade teacher, Mrs. Linda Fladeland at John Ericsson Grade School in Minneapolis, Minnesota – and it's just one of the many lessons that encouraged her love of learning.

Linda Fladeland was a third-grade student's dream of a teacher – at least to this third grader. She was upbeat, energetic and enthusiastic. She challenged us and made learning fun. It was obvious, even to a third-grader, she loved teaching.

I was an impressionable young girl, and Mrs. Fladeland **encouraged** my love for reading. When lunch break concluded, we went on adventures that stimulated our imagination with Charlotte ("Charlotte's Web"), Laura ("Little House in the Big Woods") and the Boxcar Children. This was fun.

Mrs. Fladeland **encouraged** my love of math, and gave us weekly math tests. This was not always fun, but I did learn my multiplication tables.

In addition to the academics, she also **stimulated** my love of athletics. Mrs. Fladeland was an avid sports fan and introduced me to her favorite - baseball. She loved the Minnesota Twins (especially Tony Oliva) and had us playing baseball whenever possible. This was fun.

One lesson I and every one of her students will never forget, was to not bite our fingernails. According to Mrs. Fladeland, it was a "known fact" that if you did bite your fingernails, they would no doubt stick to your appendix. You would eventually be in such pain that your appendix would need removal! Although frightening at the time, this lesson is now amusing and fun.

Mrs. Fladeland inspired me to make education a career choice, and I earned my teaching certification in secondary mathematics. Even though my mathematics degree led me to the business world rather than the academic world, I have used my teaching skills to mentor the young people that I work with.

When my working days in industry are over, it's still my goal to work and/or teach young people in some capacity. I can thank Mrs. Fladeland for instilling this passion that has endured throughout my life.

Gayle Spiess graduated from Valparaiso University in 1977 with a B.S. in Mathematics. She's worked for Lockheed Martin for 32 years, and in the late 1990s spent a total of over three months in China developing an air traffic control system for Shanghai, Nanchang and Hangzhou. Initially one of six software developers on the project, she eventually became the software lead. "Working with the Chinese on a day-to-day basis and seeing their country was invaluable," she says.

Spiess is now the Project Engineer on a program developing the next generation air traffic control system.

ALBERT "AL" STEVENS

President and CEO, Opex Corporation

Al Stevens didn't consider himself a scholar or school leader in high school, but he loved math, science and chemistry. He wanted to study engineering, but couldn't afford the tuition. That's when the school's Dean of Boys – who was also his physics and chemistry teacher – helped Stevens get a scholarship. The scholarship was worth $75, but with tuition just $32 per quarter, it helped Stevens achieve his dreams.

Looking back I have had numerous teachers that have helped and encouraged me during my school years. Several stand out and I would like to share as best I can the view of those special teachers through the eyes of a growing boy and an immature young man.

Their stories may not seem to be life-changing events. But by doing their job and adding extra help where it was needed, the influence these teachers had on me turned out to be much more important than they could ever have imagined.

My junior high experience helped me discover that I had an affinity for music. Mr. Gilley was our music and literature teacher. I recall that he often played the violin in our music class. On several occasions he played "The Flight of the Bumblebee." My heart raced as his bow would dance on the strings and produce music that was out of this world. I wanted to play like Mr. Gilley! While my parents could barely make ends meet they sacrificed so that I could take private lessons and advance my skills on the violin. I was blessed to be able to be good enough to join the Terre Haute Symphony while in high school, and hear great music performed by our orchestra as well as the guest artists. While my skills were above average, I did not personally have the ability to rise to the professional level. The orchestra experience did create an appreciation for music and a respect for those who had been gifted to be able to reach levels of professional performance that are reserved for only the best.

While music was a high point in junior high, math and most of the other subjects were not very interesting and in the eighth grade, I nearly failed math. High school was a big transition for me and a chance to "start over." Much to my surprise, the math teacher at Garfield High School taught in such a way that I understood the concepts and actually enjoyed doing the homework. I can still picture this very short lady with snow-white hair as she stood at the blackboard to teach us the next lesson and then have us review the results of the prior day's assignment. I looked forward to going to her class each day to see how well I had done as I checked my answers. Her name was Inez Kelly and she turned me around so that I loved math. This further sparked my interest in physics and chemistry, and ultimately math and science became my majors in college.

My high school physics and chemistry teacher was also the Dean of Boys. His name was Mr. Homer Powell and he made the greatest impression on me, and ultimately my future plans and direction in life. I learned a lot from his classroom instruction, but his lasting impact was to be made known just prior to graduation. While college tuition was not expensive by today's standards, I could not afford to go to Rose Hulman Institute and become an engineer. I would need to choose Indiana State where the tuition was more in line with my ability to pay. As an encouragement for me to attend Indiana State University, Mr. Powell was successful in getting me a scholarship to help with tuition. At the time I never shared my feelings with anyone about the scholarship. I felt undeserving of any scholarship. I was not a scholar. I was not in the inner circle of students that would be considered a leader in school functions. I never found out why he selected me but I have been forever grateful to a man who encouraged me by this one act.

As my name was read at graduation along with other scholarship recipients it encouraged me to do my best in furthering my education. The scholarship for $75 went a long way to cover the tuition which was $32 a quarter. No doubt this fit with God's plan in preparing me for my life's work and provided an excellent base for my career in business. I am grateful for those teachers mentioned above along with others, but the greatest impact that a schoolteacher had on my life was Mr. Powell.

I would be remiss if I did not give credit to my parents who by example taught me hard work and a set of values that I cling to this very day.

Thank you, Mr. Gilley, Mrs. Kelly and Mr. Powell, and especially to my dear mom and dad, neither of whom finished eighth grade.

Al Stevens, an Indiana State University alumnus in 1961 and 1969, was honored by the school as a Distinguished Alumni for 2001. He is the president and CEO of Opex Corporation. When he bought the financially strapped firm, it had eight employees. Today OPEX employs 500 people and is the market leader in manufacturing mail-extraction equipment. He lives in Moorestown, New Jersey.

JACK STINE

Retired COO, Northern Indiana Public Service Co.

Jack Stine was on track to become an engineer, but when a professor piqued his interest in economics, it encouraged him to test another career path – business.

Choosing a favorite teacher required me to look back more than 60 years! After considerable thought, I concluded that teachers at two different times and places were important to my late career.

First, at Fort Wayne High School in 1942 as graduation approached, several math and science teachers specifically encouraged me to consider a future in the field of engineering. This advice was an important factor in my decision to enter Purdue University that fall.

Secondly, in 1946 after a three-year break during World War 2, I returned to Purdue to complete the requirements for a BSEE (Bachelor of Science in Electrical Engineering). I still remember a course in General Economics, taught by a professor from Turkey. He presented the subject in such an interesting way that it helped to expand my career outlook beyond strictly engineering. At the earliest opportunity after graduation in 1949, in my first job I entered the part-time graduate program in business at Northwestern University. I was granted an MBA degree in 1956.

Looking back, I am sure that the interest and counsel offered by teachers had an important influence in my 40-year career at NIPSCO.

Jack Stine graduated from Fort Wayne South Side High School and earned a BSEE degree from Purdue University in

1949. After 40 years with the Northern Indiana Public Service Co., he retired as executive vice president and COO in 1989. At the time NIPSCO was the largest utility in the state of Indiana.

SHERYL STORY

Attorney

The two R's to learning are Read and Recall.

You can judge a civilization by how they treat their aged and their pets.

Only boring people are ever bored.

Katherine "Katie" Garn impressed those lessons on the students in her World and American History classes at Plymouth High School – and today, nearly 40 years later, Sheryl Story repeats them to her children and grandchildren.

Katie Garn's teachings and her approach to the world compelled me to be a history major at Valparaiso University, and to eventually become a lawyer. She taught me how to think and to pay attention to details. While it may not be truly valuable to know the name of Alexander the Great's horse, knowing all these years later that Alexander's horse was Bucephalus demonstrates how Katie created the discipline to learn. As Miss Garn would say, "Trifles make perfection, but perfection is no trifle."

While Katie Garn never married or had children, she certainly played a role in her students' development and influenced more teens than anyone in town. She was born in 1905 and lived to the age of 95, passing away in 2000. She graduated from Plymouth High School in 1923 and Indiana University in 1927. She received her master's degree from the University of Wisconsin in 1936. She came from a long line of teachers – her mother Margaret A. McFarlin taught in Donaldson and Sligo after graduating from Valparaiso Normal School.

Miss Garn was an institution at Plymouth High School. She taught me, my sister, my mother, my father, my aunt and uncles, and all my high school chums. Anyone who attended PHS from the 1930s to the 1970s will recall a story or two about her. She was a force unto herself. At less than five feet tall, she could quell the most rebellious football player with a mere peek over her glasses. She was known for traveling the world during summer breaks and sharing those experiences with her classes. She was also a notorious cat lover. Her favorite, Chrissy Bell, lived at least 21 years last I knew.

Katie did not really use a textbook, because in her opinion, no textbook covered the curriculum appropriately. Instead, she wrote what she referred to as her "contract" on five blackboards at least twice a week. Each student copied the "contract" exactly as written using a cartridge fountain pen. Katie disdained ballpoint pens as less than perfect. Many a fountain pen exploded in lockers throughout the years, ruining gym clothes, etc. Students had to retain the written contract in a three-ring binder, which Miss Garn would collect three or four times a year to review for accuracy. Aside from the historical content, she graded the notebooks on whether the proper outline format was used. *My mother, my sister, and I all still have our Katie Garn notebooks!*

Each week she also wrote "questions" on the blackboard, which students were required to record in pencil in a spiral notebook. The answers to the questions were to be handed in the morning of each test, after folding the college-ruled paper lengthwise. She allowed the class a last few minutes to study while she corrected the answers. If your name was called, you raced to her desk to pick up your answer sheet, returned to your desk and corrected the errors, and raced back to hand it back in to her. Meanwhile, she began the test without you!

All of her tests were 50 oral questions, which each student had to answer on thin-ruled loose-leaf paper. She evidently did not believe high school students were experienced enough to provide responses to essay questions, so there were none. Her grading scale was high and certainly not a bell curve! A score of 94 to 100 was an "A" – 88 to 93 was a "B" and so on. With each question worth two points, A's were difficult to come by.

Now one might conclude from my reminiscences that she was a bit of a tyrant – and she sort of was. There were, no doubt, many students who felt terrorized and recall her class with less than fond memories. But when you completed a class taught by Katie Garn, even if you received a "D," you knew more history than many others.

To this day, I often quote a few of her sayings – to my children and grandchildren. I believe she originated at least the first two. They obviously made an impact on me, as I remember them all these years later:

The two R's to learning are Read and Recall.

You can judge a civilization by how they treat their aged and their pets.

Only boring people are ever bored.

Thank you, Katie.

Born in Plymouth, Sheryl Story graduated from Plymouth High School in 1973 and earned a B.A. in history from Valparaiso University in 1977. She attended Valparaiso University School of Law for one year, and then moved to New Orleans where she earned her law degree at Loyola University School of Law.

Story has practiced law as an insurance defense litigator for Travelers, CIGNA, Zurich, and now CNA, where she is the manager of the litigation office in New Orleans. She and her husband Tom Axelrad have four children and two grandchildren.

JO YOUNG SWITZER

President, Manchester College

How many times have you seen a car with its turn signal blinking, and then watched the driver speed by without making the turn? Every time she sees a car's turn signal flashing, Jo Young Switzer waits to see whether the car actually makes the turn – and remembers with gratitude how a college communications professor used that example to teach her to think carefully.

Paul Keller, long-time professor of communication at Manchester College, taught a class called Language and Thought. Professor Keller was artful in guiding class conversations and in drawing students into levels of intellectual engagement that went far beyond what we expected of ourselves.

He asked questions that cut through to the pivotal issues. Some of his questions were broad and evocative. Others were laser-focused.

Drawing from a theoretical perspective called General Semantics, he helped us understand how many human problems begin because we do not think carefully enough about what we see. His simplest example was that of a car with its turn signal flashing. If we assume that the signal guarantees that the driver will turn as indicated, we could be in big danger – because the facts of the situation are quite limited. The turn signal is on. Our inference is that the person will turn the corner. Confusing the two can be life-threatening. The extension of this simple example is the inferences, many of them inaccurate, that we make about people, motives, and nations.

Professor Keller's gentle approach to teaching and his intense listening opened my mind and the minds of other students. He taught us the importance of realizing that people change over time, and that outdated impressions of people can lead us to miss rich opportunities for interaction. He taught us that just because things may have the same name – like "Hoosier" or "Muslim" – it didn't mean that every Hoosier or every Muslim person was like all the others.

As I wait to pull onto a highway, now 40 years later, I wait to make sure the car with the turn signal is actually turning, remembering with respect and gratitude the good teaching of Professor Paul Keller.

President Jo Young Switzer assumed the leadership of Manchester College on Dec. 1, 2004. For the previous 11 years, she served the College as vice president and dean for academic affairs.

She was born in Huntington, and graduated from Fort Wayne South Side High School. She earned a Ph.D. and master's degree in communication studies from the University of Kansas. She also has taught at Manchester College and Indiana Purdue University Fort Wayne.

She and her professor husband Dave have three grown children.

Dr. Switzer says her most treasured career accomplishments are winning the "Professor of the Year" award from the Disabled Students' Organization at Indiana University Purdue University at Fort Wayne in 1991, and being selected as President of Manchester College.

GEORGE TALIAFERRO

The "Jackie Robinson" of professional football

Called the "Jackie Robinson of professional football," George Taliaferro was the first African-American football player drafted to play in the National Football League. He says the lessons he learned from his parents and his high school swim coach helped him develop the attitude that made him a winner in life.

Every day before I left home for Roosevelt School my father and mother told me two things: "We love you" and "You must be educated."

My eighth-grade health and safety teacher Mr. William P. Swan told me every day that I could be anything I wanted to be if I had the willpower to work hard. Mr. Swan worked summers as a swim coach, and it was he who helped me develop as an all-around athlete.

I developed the attitude "Be the best that you can be" and you will inspire others to follow your lead. It worked. This is the way I have lived my life and been richly rewarded in every phase of my life.

A graduate of Gary Roosevelt High School, George Taliaferro played on Indiana University's only undefeated football team in 1945. He's also the only three-time All-America football player in the history of Indiana University.

Although he was drafted by the Chicago Bears, Taliaferro chose instead to play for the Los Angeles Dons of the All-America Football Conference. That league was more accommodating to African-American players and even though playing for the Bears was his childhood dream, Taliaferro stuck with the AAFC because he had given them his word first.

After a season with the Dons, Taliaferro played professionally for the New York Yanks, the Dallas Texans, the Baltimore Colts and the Philadelphia Eagles.

He later served as dean of students at Morgan State University and earned a master's degree in social work from Howard University. He's served as Chairman Emeritus of the Children's Organ Transplant Association and co-founded the Big Brothers/Big Sisters chapter in Bloomington, where he now lives.

GAIL TEGARDEN

Director, Lake County Court Appointed Special Advocate Association

If you were a smart, ambitious girl who lived in a small town, like Gail Tegarden, most people thought you'd be a teacher. And thanks to the smart, ambitious girls who did become teachers in her small town, Tegarden attended a big-city college and earned a law degree.

Back in my day, smart girls were kind of out of place. If you were smart, well, you could be a nurse, maybe - maybe a pharmacist. A head smarter than any boy around, the notion that I might want to leave my small Indiana town for a big-named, big-city college and a law degree, was not understandable or acceptable and certainly not encouraged. I remember still some now faceless sixth- or seventh-grade guidance counselor telling my mom that my test scores were good and I should teach. I could always teach.

I am the product of a small-town public school education. And when I made my way to the big-name, big-city college and law degree, I was many times astonished by the size – the breadth and the depth -- of my small-town public school education. I remember as I readied myself for that first airplane trip out east, my parents worried whether I was good enough, whether I was smart enough, whether I could keep up. But I was and I could and it was because, for years before me, smart girls could always teach.

And they did. From kindergarten through twelfth grade my small town public school education was highlighted by the bright minds of grown-up smart girls. These women taught me not just to read, but to understand, and not just to understand, but to think and create, to reason and to write. They introduced me to Walt Whitman and jazz music, to the Constitution and the

Renaissance, to Zen and Buddha, and to why planes fly and how angels soar.

Miss Drukamiller taught me that every once in awhile you have to work, especially if you wanted to learn to multiply. Miss Davis showed me that occasionally you had to work even a bit harder. A wonderful woman taught me how to diagram an English sentence and then how good writing could float beyond. Miss Herzog taught me how to read and a small, serious woman taught me the origins of words. I learned Latin and Russian, and how to sew and make tuna casserole, and for all of this and more I have generations of smart women to thank. Because they taught.

Bound by their times and their times' traditions, these women's choices were few. But they made a way for smart girls like me to leave the small towns, and take their first airplane ride.

Gail Tegarden is director of the Lake County Court Appointed Special Advocate (CASA) Association which is responsible for the over 2,000 Lake County children in foster care due to abuse or neglect. She also directs the Juvenile Justice Clinic.

Tegarden attended Clayton Brownlee Elementary School, McCullough Junior High School and Marion High School in Marion. She earned her bachelor's degree at Boston University and graduated from Valparaiso University School of Law, where she is an assistant professor of law.

GREGORY R. ULM

Professor Emeritus of Education, Indiana State University

Nuns have virtually disappeared from parochial schools today, but Sister Mary Lilian from the St. Joseph Convent in Tipton made a lasting impact on not only Gregory Ulm, but his brothers and sisters as well.

Sister Mary Lilian taught third, fourth and fifth grades in one room at my elementary school – St. Mary in Frankfort. She helped me understand that learning takes place in many different ways, and that self-discipline, practice and mastery of the basics are necessary precursors of creativity. She also helped me to understand what it meant to be a leader, to serve others and to "unconditionally" accept others. She nurtured a love of teaching in nearly all of my brothers and sisters – four of five entered the teaching profession. As all of us are first-generation college graduates, our successes are based on what we believe, what we value and how that helped to define our life.

Sister Mary cared for me deeply and her humor, intellect and dedication have always been a part of my frequent reflections. She would have appreciated the intent of "No child left behind," though I am certain she would argue for a different way of addressing the needs of learners.

Gregory R. Ulm graduated from Indiana State University and is professor emeritus of education there. He served as principal of the university's lab school prior to its closing in 1985 and as chair of ISU's educational leadership, administration and foundations department. He was honored with the ISU Foundation 2009 Philanthropy Award.

Now retired, he remains active at ISU by serving on dissertation committees, mentoring students and faculty, and as an Educational Leadership Advisory member. He also works on various projects to promote ISU and the College of Education.

MATTHEW R. ULM

Producer/Video editor

A loud "look-at-me!" wardrobe was only the leading edge of music teacher Judy Grimes' genius. Combined with her energy and creativity, she taught her students to express themselves and work together as a group – lessons that Matthew Ulm now realizes can lead to a lifetime of success.

Judy Grimes is a force of nature, both personally and professionally. When she walks into a room, her presence demands attention. The reason is two-fold – her attire, in the '80s, consisted of high heels, pantyhose that usually had a daring pattern, mini-skirts, blouses with shoulder pads (which only increased her larger-than-life presence) and wide, flat-brimmed hats that often had a long feather in the brim. In addition to all that, she absolutely radiated an aura of creativity, energy and vitality.

At University School in Terre Haute there was a very strong music program that started, looking back, extraordinarily early. In band you started on the recorder in the second grade and in third grade you chose your instrument. Judy convinced me that rather than going with the flashy, center-stage commanding trumpet, I should play the trombone instead. The trombone is more of a supportive instrument. Solos are rare, but there was nothing like belting out the baseline to "Working in the Coalmine" at school concerts, public appearances and during Indiana State University's Homecoming Parade.

As a student I was exposed to Judy's energetic and creative influence at a very young age and for a blessedly long time. I followed her to Jamaica to visit schools and play for students and spent my summers under her tutelage at the Creative, Musical and Theatrical Showcase. These were some of my fondest memories as a child and the lessons she taught me about expressing myself and being part of a group working towards a common goal are just as vital and important to me today. She truly gave it her all and her students reaped a magnificent reward for her efforts.

Ulm has been a producer/video editor for Stage 1 Productions in Evansville since 2001. He deals with clients, writers, photographers, talent and staff during all phases of production. Previously, he was weekend assignment editor with WTWO-TV2, the NBC affiliate in Terre Haute.

He says his most treasured accomplishment was creating a video for Navy veterans who returned the USS LST 325 from Greece.

ALEX VAGELATOS

Former editor, Lake County Star

A sixth-grade teacher who expected her students to be responsible and reliable put Alex Vagelatos on the road to adulthood.

Ms. Lynn Blandings' sixth-grade class at John H. Vohr Elementary School in Gary was the first in which I recognized being treated as something more than a child. She expected us to do good work, and be responsible and reliable without much oversight from her. It may seem like a small thing, but I now realize it was my gateway into being a grown-up.

Alex Vagelatos graduated from Horace Mann High School in Gary and from Indiana University with degrees in journalism and English. He was a newspaper and magazine editor in Indiana and Michigan, and is currently the marketing director for the University of Wisconsin-Milwaukee School of Education.

SALVADOR VASQUEZ

Judge, Superior Court of Lake County

Dorothy had to go all the way to Oz to learn there's no place like home. One of Salvador Vasquez' college professors knew the truth of that adage – and challenged him to come back home after he earned a law degree. Vasquez accepted that challenge – and has often passed his mentor's message on to others.

It is with great respect that I write these words in honor of my friend and mentor, Mr. Martin Becerra, Jr. Martin passed away on March 11, 1999. He was a true educator in every sense of the term.

Martin was an educator at Indiana University Northwest (IUN) in the Bilingual Education Department. While I never took any of his courses since my major was History and Political Science, that didn't prevent him from reaching out to me and treating me as though I had enrolled in many of his classes. His influence on me as an educator and counselor affects me to this day.

Martin was born in Mexico and came to the United States at an early age. He managed to learn English and eventually earn a Master's degree (I believe in English). My parents were also born in Mexico and came to the United States during their late teens. Due in part to their age at the time of immigration, they never had the opportunity to seek any formal education in this country. Neither one of my parents managed to obtain a high school education. They divorced when I was graduating from high school and my father moved back to Mexico.

Against this backdrop, seeking a college education was an enormous undertaking for me. I met Martin soon after enrolling at IUN. He was to become my mentor, friend, and father figure. He helped me to keep my focus and to follow my heart and dreams. If I had any problems or issues, I always knew that I could turn to Martin for guidance and inspiration.

Martin cared about Northwest Indiana. Where it has been and where it's going. He deeply cared about issues of fairness and equal treatment when it came to our population with its deep ethnic and racial makeup. He truly believed that individuals and individual effort could make a difference in our way of life. He often spoke of the perils of apathy and complacency.

His most lasting legacy with me came when I was nearing graduation from IUN. I had applied to law school and was yet undecided on what to do and/or where to attend. Of course, I sought his guidance and wisdom. I recall a conversation where he pointed out that many of Northwest Indiana's most talented students and future leaders will obtain their education and seek their opportunities elsewhere. He indicated that regardless of the many opportunities for employment, income or advancement that may exist in other parts of Indiana or the United States, we need these people to come back to the Northwest Indiana region and make a difference here at home. He would say that anyone could complain about any situation. The true challenge will be the desire to do something about it.

He only asked that I consider this when making my decisions on career and employment upon graduation. He never asked me to commit.

I graduated from IUN in 1988. Sure enough when I graduated from Indiana University School of Law in Bloomington in 1991, I returned to Northwest Indiana to practice law and hopefully, make a difference.

As I was contemplating a decision on whether to seek a judicial appointment, I recalled Martin's challenge to me. When he died in 1999, I wept uncontrollably.

I certainly hope that I continue to seek and fulfill this challenge. It is a message that I have repeated often to others.

A graduate of Indiana University Northwest and the Indiana University School of Law in Bloomington, Salvador Vasquez was appointed Judge in the Superior Court of Lake County in June 2003.

ALEX VRACIU

Navy Cross recipient

The lasting legacy of Lieutenant Commander Edward "Butch" O'Hare – the U.S. Navy's first flying ace and Medal of Honor recipient in World War 2 – was assured when Chicago's Orchard Depot Airport was renamed in his honor. Japanese bombers shot his aircraft down on November 26, 1943. It was never recovered. But before he gave his life for his country, O'Hare taught everything he knew to his wingman – Alex Vraciu.

Lieutenant Commander Butch O'Hare was part of an exceptional breed of early World War 2 carrier fighter pilots who helped hold the line against Japan until America's might produced all the tools necessary to roll back the carpet in the Pacific. Butch's distinguished Ace-in-a-day performance in February 1942 on the old carrier Lexington, which earned him the Medal of Honor, provided a much-needed boost to the Navy and home-front morale.

Butch was a natural-born leader who easily instilled learning and confidence in his squadron pilots, primarily stressing gunner and teamwork. He had a quiet demeanor – never said much – but then, he never had to. We listened to him because of his experience and service reputation. Having been his wingman, and later section leader in his division, I consider myself most fortunate to have learned my trade from this remarkable man.

Having one's first combat while flying wing on this kind of leader definitely gives one the necessary confidence to fly competition-smart against a highly dedicated enemy. Without even thinking, I found myself time and again using techniques that he advised, like developing a swivel neck, looking back over my shoulder before commencing a run, conserving fuel and ammunition, and firing close and aiming at the wing root of the enemy plane.

Alex Vraciu graduated from East Chicago Washington High School in 1937 and won a scholarship to DePauw University. After graduating he enlisted in the U.S. Navy in June 1941, and was commissioned a naval aviator in August 1942. He shot down his first enemy aircraft at Wake Island in October 1943. In June 1944 he shot down six enemy bombers in just eight minutes, a feat known as the "Great Marianas Turkey Shoot." He was the Navy's leading ace for four months in 1944 and ended World War 2 as the fourth-ranking Naval Ace, having shot down 19 enemy aircraft and destroyed 21 more on the ground.

Vraciu was awarded the Navy Cross, Distinguished Flying Cross and Air Medal.

After post-war staff duty in the Navy Department, Naval Post-Graduate School and shipboard duty, he was Commanding Officer of Fighter Squadron 51. He retired from the U.S. Navy in 1964 and began a career in banking. Now retired, the father of five lives in Danville, California.

EUGENE G. WHITE

Superintendent, Indianapolis Public Schools

Boys like Dr. Eugene White who grow up in single-parent homes need a male role model. For Dr. White, that man was his principal at South Girard High School in Phenix City, Alabama.

Mr. Loyld Bowie was such a dynamic leader and a man who demonstrated the values and attributes missing in the lives of single-parent boys like me. He was totally committed to excellence and he wanted each of us to be the best that we could be.

Mr. Bowie would often say that "our school might not be the best school in the world, but we had to make sure that it was the best school that we knew." He did not accept excuses and he daily set an example of courage, determination and scholarship.

We knew he loved each of us and that he would do everything possible to help us. He was a wonderful educator and a great man. I will always remember Mr. Bowie.

Dr. Eugene G. White was born in Phenix City, Alabama, to a 17-year-old single mother. He was the first person in his family to graduate from high school, where he excelled in football, basketball and baseball. He was a starting member of the 1966 Alabama State Championship Basketball team and accepted a basketball scholarship to Alabama A&M University. He received Ed.D. and Ed.S. degrees from Ball State University, an M.S. from the University of Tennessee and a B.S. from Alabama A&M University.

Dr. White was a teacher, coach and school administrator in the Fort Wayne Community Schools for 19 years. He was the first African-American high school principal in the Fort Wayne Community Schools, where he served as principal of Wayne High School from 1985 to 1990. In 1990 he became the first African-American high school principal of North Central High School in Indianapolis, serving until 1992. He was Deputy Superintendent of the Indianapolis Public Schools from July 1992 to January 1994. He served as the Superintendent of the Metropolitan School District of Washington Township for 11 years. In 2005, Dr. White was named Superintendent of the state's largest school district. He was named Indiana Superintendent of the Year in 2002 and 2009.

REV. WARREN W. WIERSBE

Bible teacher, author and conference speaker

A casual conversation with his sixth-grade teacher set Warren Wiersbe on his life's path – a path that's led to publishing over 160 books! At the 2002 Christian Booksellers Convention, he was awarded the "Gold Medallion Lifetime Achievement Award" by the Evangelical Christian Publishers Association.

The first of my favorite teachers is Marie Jablonski who taught sixth grade at Washington Elementary School in East Chicago. Each Friday, she would ask us to write a one-page essay about anything that happened that week, which I was happy to do because I liked to write. Unknown to me, she kept my little essays. When I was about to go into Junior High (I guess it's called Middle School now), Miss Jablonski called me aside and showed me her file of my essays. "I want you to do a lot of reading," she said, "and also a lot of writing. I think that's where your future lies." It was like an oracle from heaven. Just thinking about it brings tears to my eyes.

Well, it overwhelmed me, but I took her advice. Of course, I'd been a steady patron at the public library since third grade, but now I could use the school library in that beautiful new building. And here's where teacher number two comes in – Ruth Lucas, the school librarian. Well, she wasn't really a teacher, but technically was on the faculty. My sister Doris was a "library assistant," so I had a safe "in" with Miss Lucas. I would drop into the library after school and, as busy as she was, she would take time to chat with me about books and reading. She recommended good books to me and steered me away from the ones I didn't need. She even talked with me about the books that she was reading and why she was reading them. She especially steered me towards biography and autobiography, which has been my favorite kind of reading ever since. When I shared my own plans for writing, she encouraged me and recommended books to help me.

I suppose I could also include Mr. Altenderfer, the print shop instructor. I took print shop several years and was on the staff of the school newspaper, the Anvil. Mr. Altenderfer taught me how to read proofs and use the proper proof marks when correcting them. I don't know how many proofs I've read over the past 50 years. He also clued me in on the making and binding of books. I was useless as a pressman, but when it came to words on paper, I was in my glory.

Over the years, the good Lord has helped me write and publish over 160 books, many of which have been translated into other languages. I've also written for (or edited) several magazines, and it's been a great life – and fun! And it started with a casual conversation with Miss Jablonski when I was in sixth grade. Miracles still happen.

Warren Wiersbe was converted to Christ in 1945 at a Youth for Christ rally where Billy Graham was the speaker in his hometown of East Chicago. He studied at Indiana University and Roosevelt University in Chicago, and in 1953 received a Bachelor of Theology degree from Northern Baptist Seminary then in Chicago.

He has served as pastor of Central Baptist Church in East Chicago, and Calvary Baptist Church in Covington, Kentucky. He was also director of the literature division and editor of "YFC Magazine" now "Campus Life" at Youth for Christ International in Wheaton, Illinois.

From 1971 to 1978 he was the senior minister at The Moody Church in Chicago where he moderated the radio show "Songs in the Night." From 1980 to 1989 Rev. Wiersbe hosted the "Back to the Bible Broadcast" in Lincoln Nebraska, where he now lives.

DONALD R. YEOMAN

Indiana Superintendent of the Year 2000

Practice, practice, practice. That's the lesson Donald Yeoman learned from his high school band teacher – and it's motivated him ever since.

I was a freshman in the Hebron High School band and had experienced a series of band directors over the years who had simply maintained the status quo. Then Joe Bondi came to town as band director with his humor, musical skill, vision, and drive to help kids make beautiful music. He challenged us to set goals way beyond our imagination, and he helped us achieve at higher and higher levels in a process of what is known today as "continuous quality improvement."

He started our first jazz band and introduced us to first-rate jazz composers. He designed marching shows for basketball games, and we amazed our parents and our community on Friday nights when we delivered exciting performances of his shows. He entered us in parade competitions, and he took us to Purdue's Band Day to perform with one of the nation's top performing bands. All along the way he made our experience with him the best part of our day. My friends and I lived for that hour in band where we were acknowledged as a key member of his organization, challenged to excel, and expected to shine.

One day a student asked him how much we should practice. He said, "If you don't practice today, you will know it. If you don't practice today and tomorrow, your mother will know it. If you don't practice all week, the audience will know it."

I have always remembered his words that day, and I have always prepared so that I deliver my best to the world. Joe's vision, passion and skill as a musician and educator, and his special humor and wit motivated lots of students over the years. I have been a school superintendent for many years now, and each time I hire a teacher I look for another Joe Bondi. To me, he is the model for our nation's future educators, and I am proud to have been his student so many years ago.

Now superintendent of schools in Chelmsford, Massachusetts, Dr. Donald Yeoman was named Indiana Superintendent of the Year in 2000, and served as president of the Indiana Association of Public School Superintendents in 2004.

MARY YORKE

President, Munster School Board

A teacher who made her stretch and reach and succeed, a teacher she calls beyond "the best," is the teacher who inspired Mary Yorke.

From day one he was intimidating. He seemed to know so much. Every word was filled with knowledge. It wasn't the typical class where the teacher read from the book or read the notes that he had already provided you. Actually, I was fascinated by what he knew. Some teachers analyze their audiences and some have no clue what their audiences would be interested in. He definitely knew what his audience would be baited by. I was hooked by his linguistics class, and I didn't even know I was interested in the topic.

Robert Nichols from Purdue Calumet University was the epitome of an honored teacher. Because he knew that everything he said was important, we, his students, realized the same. Sometimes teachers are driven by outside factors - student grumblings, principals' preferences, parental complaints. But once in awhile the gods give you a teacher, male or female, who believes deeply in teaching, and you know that you are being educated, that someone is giving you information that you can cherish forever, that you want to work harder.

And so it was in Nichols' linguistics class and also in the second class I took from him. I chose this class because I wanted to sit and listen to a true educator once more. It was a class in Chaucer and we read the "Canterbury Tales" in Middle English, a challenge of gigantic proportions. I was teaching five classes myself, coaching speech and caring for an ailing mom. I knew that I couldn't meet his expectations, so I asked to audit the class, and then because *he* was the teacher, I read every assignment, even 60 pages of Middle English each week.

Educators, of the highest quality, make you stretch and reach and succeed.

I took all of the Chaucer tests and even ventured to volunteer in class. You are probably thinking - why the heck didn't she take the class for credit? The only answer I have is that I didn't want to disappoint this educator. I guess subconsciously I needed an excuse for not being my best in his class.

Sometimes in life we run into a friend of whom we say "she's the best." Or perhaps you have heard people say about their doctor or dentist or lawyer, "I have the best doctor in northwest Indiana." Or maybe you have heard a friend say, "My mom is the best."

Is there a word that ever goes beyond "the best"? And what would that word be? T. S. Eliot in describing the birth of Christ tried the opposite tack. Instead of conjuring up every possible adjective to describe that momentous birth, Eliot simply said that "it was satisfactory." Robert Nichols as an educator was "totally satisfactory." As a learner, I have never been more satisfied.

Become a teacher and you will understand satisfaction.

Mary Yorke retired after teaching senior English at Munster High School for 25 years. She also coached the school's speech and debate team. Mrs. Yorke is now president of the Munster School Board.